Four Wheels Through Eurasia

Pamela Collier

ISBN-13: 978-1502462923

ISBN-10: 1502462923

All photographs, maps and diagrams in this publication are the work of the author and her husband.

Although many of the towns mentioned here have changed their names or spelling over the decades, it has been decided to keep the flavour of the original narrative by retaining the forms used at the time of the journey.

Details of other books by these authors are available on the Collier Creations website:

http://colliercreations.weebly.com

Contents

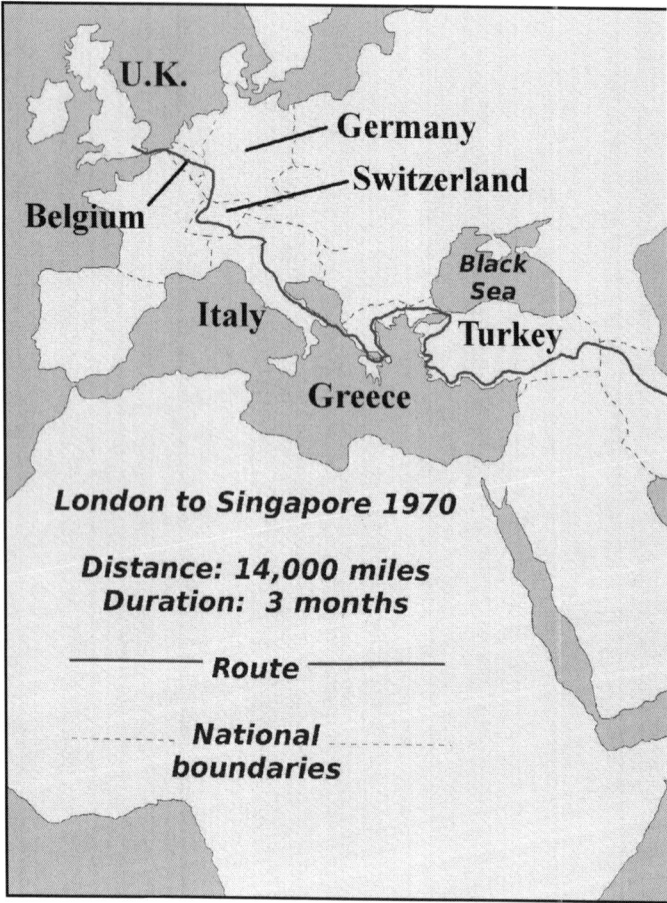

U.K.

Germany

Switzerland

Belgium

Black
Sea

Italy

Turkey

Greece

London to Singapore 1970

Distance: 14,000 miles
Duration: 3 months

———— Route ————

·········· National ··········
boundaries

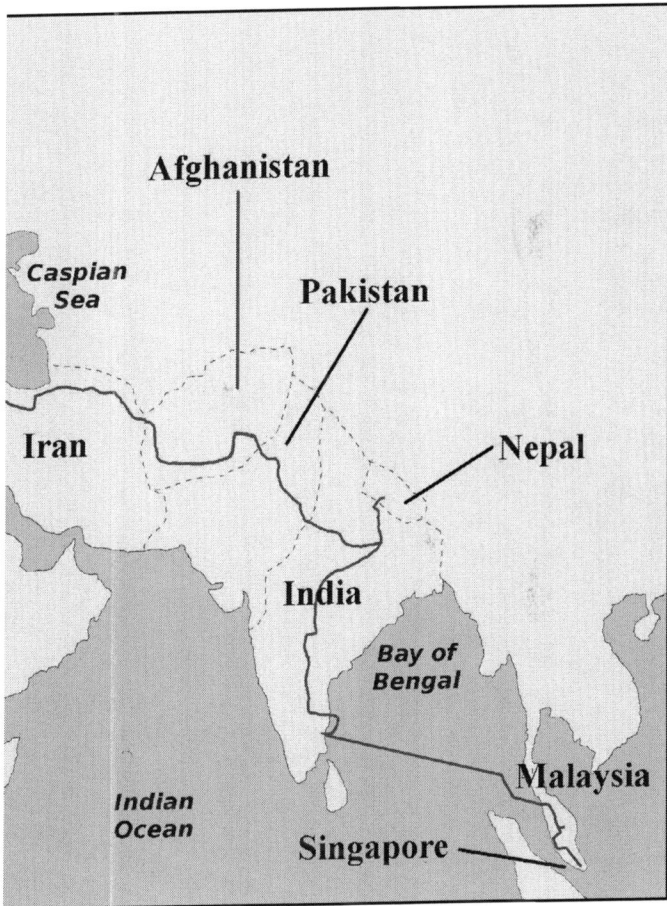

Afghanistan

Caspian
Sea

Pakistan

Iran

Nepal

India

Bay of
Bengal

Indian
Ocean

Malaysia

Singapore

Chapter 1

Gearing Up

There are many types of addiction to which people are subject today. But perhaps the strangest of them was that of my husband, Mike. From his teenage years he was compulsively drawn to one thing – modifying, maintaining and driving Bedford vans. He loved to pile such a vehicle full of people and camping equipment, to roam the British countryside in search of adventure. Eventually, these activities evolved into a plan to drive a Bedford CA van across the world from London to Singapore, possibly to be followed by working as an engineer in the East. He started recruiting other young men for this expedition, and three showed enthusiasm for being part of the project.

But the process was cataclysmically terminated, when he regretfully admitted to his confederates that there would be no room for them.

"Sorry guys. But you see it's like this... Actually the fact is... Well you see... What I mean to say is this..."

"Get on with it, Mike! What's the problem?"

"Not really a problem. Not at all, actually.... quite the opposite."

"Well, then, what's the matter?"

"You see, I've met a rather special girl - fallen in love with her - and we will soon get married. So I'm really sorry - but this is going to be a two-person show from now on. Pam will be my co-driver."

They took it stoically, like the men they were, and even offered their congratulations to us both.

And that is where I became part of the plan!

Following our marriage, we spent the first half of 1970 working furiously on converting the van into a suitable home and refuge for the 20,000 mile safari across some of

the world's wildest places. Additionally, there was a host
of peripheral matters to be settled before we could even
leave the coast of England.

The full complement of the expedition's members

Obviously a high-priority question was that of the route.
The only fixed points were London at the start, and
Singapore as the destination. We wanted as much
exposure to new cultures and environments as possible,
and therefore tried to minimise the number of boat trips –
although we accepted that some stretches of water would
have to be crossed.

At that time Russia seemed to be an unacceptable country to negotiate, and so we concluded that we must definitely pass through India. To reach there would involve travelling through several countries of the Middle East. Thus we decided that Turkey must be on the route, and having looked at ways out of that country through Syria, Iraq or Iran, we decided the last one would be preferable. From the south of Iran it was possible to drive into Pakistan, but the lure of the name "Afghanistan" made us keen to pass through that unknown and mysterious land. So we plumped for the northern route through Iran, despite warnings that road-building was still in progress.

To reach Turkey, the obvious road was through Austria, Yugoslavia and Bulgaria – but both of us had in our student days independently taken the long dreary road through Yugoslavia. Thus we looked for a more interesting way to go. We found that if we drove down the length of Italy, we could take an overnight ferry to the north of Greece, from where we could eventually come out into Turkey.

There still remained the question of getting from India to Singapore. At first we considered driving through Burma, but several reports indicated that the government there would only allow pairs of four-wheel-drive vehicles, because of the parlous state of the river crossings – and that they required a cash deposit of twice the vehicle's value before one could enter the country. Looking, instead, at ways out of India by ship, we considered sailing from Calcutta in the north or Madras in the south. The P & O line operated a bi-weekly ship from Madras to Malaysia, which seemed to be the quickest and cheapest way of crossing the Bay of Bengal – and so we booked places on the vessel for us and our van.

Having covered the major components of the trip, the final question was where to cross the English Channel. We chose the Dover to Ostend ferry, which would lead us onto the major motorways into Germany, and then south to Switzerland.

After reaching our conclusions, we spent many interesting hours in bookshops obtaining maps to cover all stages of the route.

****

The Bedford van was an empty shell when Mike bought it, and so the first modification was to add side windows, obtained from a scrap yard. We fitted two benches, in the standard camper style, which could be converted to a double bed at night by lowering a central table, and covering it with cushions. Just inside the rear door, we installed a two-ring gas cooker, and a fitting for a gaslight. Inside the cabin a large freshwater tank would supply our needs on the desert parts of the trip.

Mike's previous experience with this Bedford model had indicated a possible weakness in the gearbox, since one had failed on a previous trip to Scotland. Also, there was a strange rattling noise from the box when we were travelling downhill. After consulting local dealers, who could not explain this phenomenon, we decided that the best answer was to carry a spare gearbox. Another trip to a breaker's yard, and we had acquired a working piece of equipment, which Mike then mounted on special brackets under the van.

Expecting that the engine would have to face harsh environments and uncertain fuel, we decided that it should be decarbonised before departure. After he had removed the cylinder head, cleaned the surfaces and reground the valves, Mike was in the process of reassembling when he ran into trouble. While tightening one of the head studs he felt the thread strip, and realised that he had used the wrong length of stud. It would be impossible to remove the item without painstakingly drilling it out – and so philosophically he decided to trust all the other studs to carry the stress. We hoped we would not have to do a decoke in the middle of some remote desert!

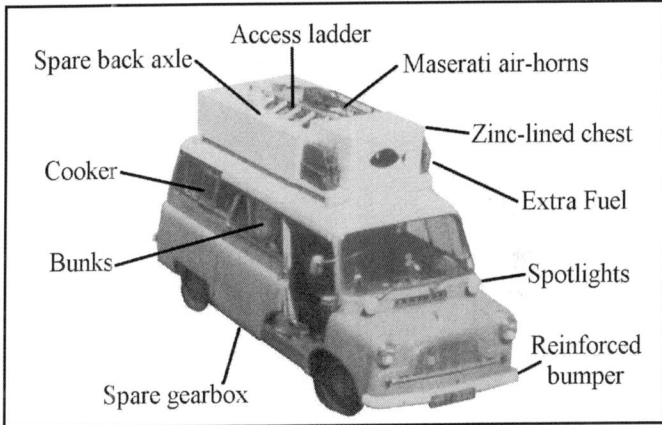

Another possible cause of breakdown could be the components of the back axle - bearings, half-shafts or differential. Having obtained a complete two-metre long axle, the dilemma was how to carry it. In the end, we built a large wooden open box on the roof, containing lockers for the many spare parts, including the axle. A zinc-lined trunk which had been in Mike's family for generations, and probably originated in India, was then mounted over the cab to provide storage for our clothes away from dust and bugs.

Realising that we might be spending nights in very hot locations, we made a structure of four poles which could be erected on the roof, so that a mosquito-net could enable us to sleep up there.

****

Security was the issue uppermost in our minds as we envisaged the plethora of countries and through which we would be passing. First, Mike went to a builders' merchant to purchase a sheet of the steel grid used in reinforcing concrete. This was cut to size and fitted inside the windows, as a deterrent to smash-and-grab enthusiasts.

We then bought a pair of dual-tone Maserati air-horns, looking like miniature trombones and powered by a tiny compressor. When we tested these in suburban south London, the windows of the houses around seemed to vibrate, satisfying us that these horns were adequate to give warning of our approach. Mike designed a circuit connected to the door switches, so that any intruder would activate these high-decibel music-makers mounted on the roof.

Regarding the carrying of money, we decided on a mixture of Travellers' Cheques and cash, but where to store these safely was a question. This was resolved by having a steel safe, of quarter-inch thick metal, bolted into a hole in the floor of the vehicle, giving us peace of mind about the security of our documents.

****

Before even leaving England, one of Mike's first introductions to the culture of Central Asia took place when he knocked on the door of an imposing Georgian house in London's West End. The brass plate proclaimed that this was the Embassy of Afghanistan. Eventually the door opened slowly, and Mike was welcomed by a black beard below unblinking brown eyes - and silence.

"Good morning - I would like to apply for a visa for Afghanistan," Mike announced, with a smile.

The reply took the form of the white-turbaned gentleman turning on his heel, and walking back down a long corridor. Mike inferred that he was to follow, and as he did so he passed several offices occupied by clones of his guide. It was obviously the Festival of Non-Smiling in Afghanistan at that time. Arriving at an office, Mike encountered another hirsute man, who looked at Mike quizzically. There was no opportunity to sit down - partly because there were no chairs and also because of no such invitation. After placing our passports and application forms on the table, Mike waited and watched a careful scrutiny of the paperwork by the hawk-eyed official. Eventually, communication was established.

"Why you want to go Afghanistan?"

"My wife and I are travelling through Central Asia on our way to Singapore."

A grunt of acknowledgement.

"Come next week this time," was the laconic dismissal.

Leaving our precious documents on the table, Mike retraced his steps through the building, where the level of levity did not appear to have increased, and was ejected through the front door.

Seven days later the procedure was repeated, and Mike received our passports complete with ornate Arabic visas from the same office. These were handed over in duly solemn silence, making us eligible to enter the mystical land of Afghanistan.

****

The question of rations absorbed us for many hours, since our storage space would be severely limited. Although for the first two or three weeks of the journey we expected to buy food easily, we were not so sure about availability after that. Probably bread and rice could be bought everywhere, together with some form of fruit and vegetables.

What was more uncertain was the provision of meat that was edible. In the end, we provided ourselves with a "protein survival kit", consisting of one tin of meat and one vacuum pack of bacon for each week of the journey ahead.

*********.

As the time for departure drew near, we made a round of farewell visits to family and friends. Arrangements had been made for us to pick up post from about four cities on our journey, and we promised faithfully to send postcards back as frequently as possible. A thorough final check of the vehicle, inventory and documents was made.

At last the day came. A small convoy, containing family members, escorted us to Dover, where hugs and tears saw us on our way.

Chapter 2
European Dash

The sun shone as the famous white cliffs of Dover receded into oblivion. We turned our backs on England, and looked over the bows of the "Artevelde" ferry towards France which was already silhouetted against a stormy sky. As we neared the European coast, flames shot from a factory chimney. We turned northward. Towns and sand-dunes passed like a kaleidoscope interrupted by the occasional sheltered harbour where cranes stood in ranks, as though awaiting inspection. On reaching the coast of Belgium, the ferry rolled violently, as we momentarily turned back towards the open sea. Spray shot over the bows, showering us with mid-summer iciness.

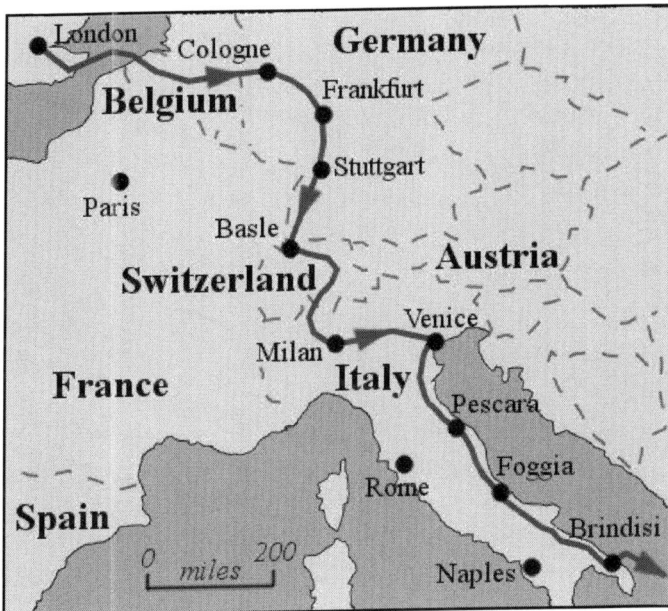

The Artevelde went into reverse to squeeze into the narrow harbour entrance at Ostend. Crockery smashed as the boat rolled, and the wind howled round the funnel as the craft perpetually heeled to starboard. Waves broke heavily against the breakwater, and the boat, having drifted too far to leeward, went forward again. This time the manoeuvre was successful, and we climbed down to the vehicle deck to find our van.

Soon we were rolling through the Belgian countryside, acutely aware of the need to "Keep right", and gradually adjusting to anti-clockwise roundabouts and overtaking on the left. We knew that we would be driving on this side of the road for many weeks, until we entered regions in Asia where the Union Jack had once flown. The countryside was flat with evidence of dairy farming, until we entered Brussels. After a quick glimpse of the Atomium, we were on our way to Louvain and Liege, while the Belgian rain welcomed us generously.

Approaching the German border, we found that the road improved considerably. At the Aachen crossing point, the immigration official was too cosy in his box to venture into the downpour. He simply peered at us, and shouted.

"Wo gehen Sie?"

"Singapore," Mike shouted back facetiously.

"Was?"

"Die Schweiz!"

With a nod he passed us through, obviously more familiar with people travelling to Switzerland, rather than to the extremities of Asia.

After a night at a pleasant campsite situated in a valley, we enjoyed the fastest day on the whole three-month trip. Cologne, Frankfurt, Mannheim, Karlsruhe and Freiburg were all by-passed on the superb German autobahn. We caught flashes of the Rhine, as it wound its way past forested hillsides with Gothic castles standing romantically in the pine trees. The great industrial towns with their chimneys and flat blocks were exchanged for small villages perched on the hillsides as we neared and crossed the Swiss border.

We found a scenic campsite near the village of Muhlehof, which consisted of a few rambling detached houses brightened by window boxes of geraniums. The following night found us camping on a small peninsular on Lake Lucerne, with the opportunity of a hike up the steep track behind the chair-lift, rewarding us with an inspiring panorama of the lakes and mountains.

****

Our exit from Switzerland involved the long, steep drive up the St Gotthard Pass, where patches of snow were still lying. After negotiating several tunnels, we began the descent, while at the same time the temperature began to rise. Soon the villages looked more Italian in architecture and character, and the road was bordered by tree-covered mountain slopes.

As the road dropped increasingly fast, we found that our van appeared to be slowing down, while simultaneously we felt that someone must be smoking in the neighbourhood. Eventually we had to pull off the road, since something was obviously wrong. As we jumped out, we were greeted with spirals of grey smoke rising from the back wheels. A quick inspection showed that it would have been quite possible to fry eggs on the brake drums, but thankfully they were not red hot. It appeared that the unexpected heat had caused the Bedford hydraulic system to expand and lock the brakes hard on. Putting on his overalls, Mike spent an uncomfortably hot hour under the vehicle, releasing some of the fluid in the brake system, and then adding large quantities of fluid to his own system to aid his recovery. The whole operation seemed to solve the problem, at least for the moment. A lovely campsite in Bellinzona gave us the chance for a long walk up to the Ai Castelli, Three Castles, where we were rewarded with ancient structures, grand views of Lake Maggiore and welcome ice-creams.

Having crossed the Italian frontier near Lake Como, we sped along the fine autostrade motorways through the north of the country, passing Milan, Brescia and Verona, in the last of which we saw at least two gentlemen! Repeated use of our red warning triangle became necessary as the engine began to overheat and the brakes continually seized up. But despite these interruptions, we made it in one day to Mestre, the town in the suburbs of Venice, where we found a strange little campsite consisting of a small courtyard with a stylish barn.

From there we roamed the streets and waterways of the canal city. Wandering around St Mark's square we were intrigued by the artists displaying their varied wares. A group of sailors in tropical attire tried to catch the attention of a blonde girl at the back of a sightseeing party, but a middle-aged woman put her arm protectively around the maiden, and the hopefuls turned their attention elsewhere.

The tall Venetian houses looked rather tired, and the gondolas a relic of a past age - it seemed the city was trying unsuccessfully to recapture its former glory. The Grand Canal was impressively busy with a mass of different vessels, and the temptations of the odours from the pizza shops in the alleyways proved too much to resist. Once darkness fell, the centre became magical with lilting classical melodies floating across the squares, and white-coated waiters flitting between the tables.

By this time, Mike realised that we had a serious problem with the brake system on the van, since whenever the air temperature rose, the pressure in the hydraulic system increased until the vehicle was immobile. So, back at the campsite, he put aside his favourite novel and immersed himself in the workshop manual for the Bedford CA van. After intense scrutiny of the pages, he found a short note to the effect that if the master cylinder push-rod were not adjusted precisely, then the pressure release hole would be blocked, resulting in brake seizure. So Mike crawled into the sandy Italian dirt under the vehicle, and spent a not-to-be-repeated session keeping the sweat and oil out of his eyes while wielding the slimy spanners. Not exactly the siesta he would have chosen! Happily the procedure worked, and for the next three months there was no repeat of the brake problem.

****

Leaving this fascinating city, we began the long slow journey down the east coast of Italy. After the flat, straight motorways of the north, it was pleasant to join slower winding roads through villages and little towns. Many of these were heavily tree-lined, and as we emerged from these leafy tunnels we were met by great expanses of maize, vineyards, orchards of rosy peaches, and occasional fields of sunflowers. Protruding from the coastal plain were outcrops of rock, often revealing castles or small villages perched on their summits.

Wayside stall in southern Italy

As we waited at one railway crossing, a grey-haired old man cycled up to an electric water pump, filled a large can, and then rode away with the vessel balanced on the handlebars. We wondered how many times a day he made this journey, and how far it was to his home.

Campsites were scenic and facilities good as we continued south, but we were getting weary of the flat coastal plain. Suddenly, near Pesaro, the road began to climb, and we looked out onto a shimmering sea where the coast was covered in rows of olive trees, fields of bamboo and the occasional palm-tree.

In one small village I approached a stall that seemed well stocked with edible provisions, but the one item I wanted was not in evidence. After failing to communicate verbally with the woman in charge, I had to resort to my vast experience of studying O-level art by using a piece of wrapping paper to depict a hen sitting on a nest of eggs. This was received with squawks of understanding, and soon a tray of fresh, large eggs was produced.

A feeling of the orient at the heel of Italy

As we journeyed further south we felt that the architecture began to have an eastern flavour. Several times we looked at a vista of wedding-cake towns nestling on the hillsides, with the occasional rich dome contrasting with the blanched walls and flat roofs.

Around Andria the road turned inland, and the heat increased. The fields were bounded by dry stone walls, enclosing groves of olive trees whose forked trunks, gnarled and twisted, resembled witches bending over cauldrons.

Eventually we reached Brindisi, the last stop on the Italian foot - and from which we would kick off to Greece. Dusk was falling as we joined the stream of cars on the quay, pointing towards the yawning gap in the stern of the "Appia", the ferry that would take us overnight to the next stage of our trip. An hour later, the van had been squeezed into the lower-deck car park of the ship, and we went above to find our "aircraft seats" in which to spend the night. The lights of the land of the Caesars receded slowly as we slumbered.

Chapter 3
Hellenic Hop

The morning dawned mistily, and through the haze we saw the island of Corfu loom up. Soon the "Appia" was moored at the quayside in bright sunshine, and vehicles for the island streamed off.

We remained on board, planning to land on the mainland, and the ship soon continued her voyage. Several hours later we drove out of the stern onto the pier at Igoumenitsa at the northern end of Greece's western coast.

Within minutes of leaving the town, the road climbed steeply, and we were soon surrounded by towering peaks, and looking down into deep valleys. There was little sign of habitation, and virtually no traffic on the road apart from donkeys, which were mainly ridden side-saddle. Our road was taking us directly inland to the town of Ioanina, from where we could take the main route southwards towards the Peloponnese on the far side of the Gulf of Corinth.

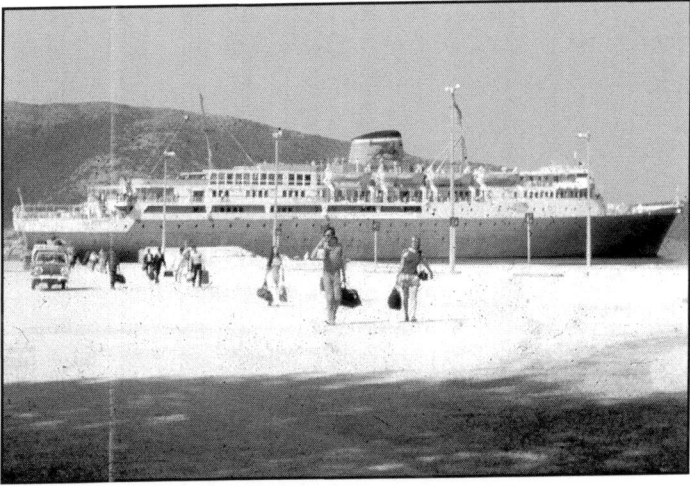

Disembarking from the "Appia" onto Greek soil

In the midst of this majestic mountain scenery, the Bedford decided that life was getting too hot for it. With a throaty roar the radiator boiled over, and added a small river of brown water to the dusty road. After giving the engine a sufficient rest to cool down, Mike removed the radiator grille on the front of the car to improve the cooling. And so for the next 10,000 miles our van would have a gaping mouth at the front - but at least it seemed to solve our overheating issue. While we waited in the scorching sun, we refreshed ourselves with dripping slices of melon.

We drove on into the evening, and at one point stopped to buy a water-melon from a huge pile by the roadside. The locals were so amused that they gave us another one free of charge. The glorious sunset accentuated the amazing colours of the rocks in the ragged mountains around.

As night fell we arrived at the coast near Patras, and a car-ferry took us in the gloaming from the mainland of Greece to the Peloponnese peninsular which forms the southern half of the country. We arrived at the other side in complete darkness, but managed to find the intended campsite on the Athens road, even though it was pitch black around us.

Cooling measures for the van - and for the drivers

We awoke to the sound of cicadas in the trees, and looked out onto the clear waters of the Gulf of Corinth, which beckoned invitingly. Across the crystal surface we saw the misty mountains that we had crossed the previous day. After eating, swimming and reading, we set out by foot in the late afternoon up a nearby hill, taking our telescope with us. From that vantage point we could see small boats out on the Gulf, and further north in the haze the major massif of central Greece.

By this time the van needed a minor service, and so Mike as chief mechanic of the expedition, clad in swimming trunks and armed with grease gun, crawled under the chassis to check and lubricate. The gearbox was still making strange sounds, but he decided it was not time to swap it with the spare one underneath the van. Little did we know that for many weeks we would journey onward with the same gearbox making the same sounds! The cause of the cacophony was never determined.

****

The Corinth Canal providing a valuable short-cut

Our next objective was the ancient city of Corinth. To save cash we tried to avoid the expensive toll roads, but soon discovered that the alternative routes were slow and twisty. Reluctantly we agreed to travel the more costly way, and made much faster progress. In the distance we could see the rocky promontory of ancient Corinth crowned with the ruined city, but initially we by-passed it in search of the Corinth Canal. This amazing engineering feat was built in 1893 by a team of French engineers, to link the Adriatic and Aegean seas. The waterway overcame the need for ships to navigate the treacherous waters around the Peloponnese.

We then headed up the stony road which climbed steeply towards the historic city. We passed a shepherd who was watering his sheep at a spring, just as his ancestors would have done from time immemorial. On rounding a bend, we were confronted by the walls of old Corinth, now a relic of a former glorious age.

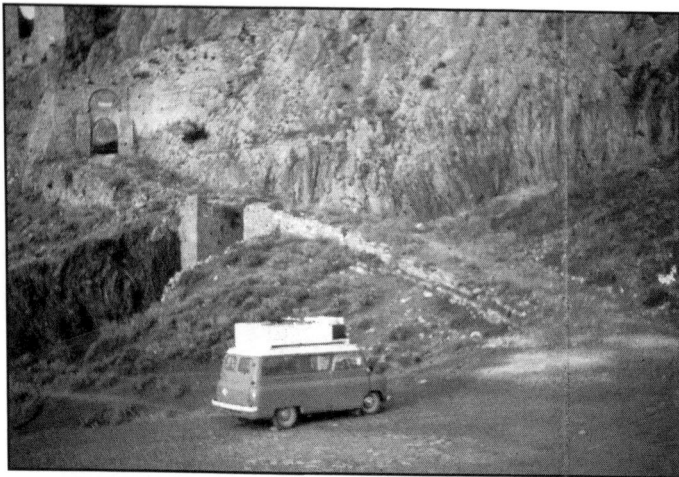

At the gates of ancient Corinth

Donning rucksacks and boots, we started the climb through the first of the three gates of the acropolis, and up the remains of the steep streets until the final gate opened into the ruined temple of Aphrodite. The Acrocorinthus stood 1857 feet above the Gulf, and from this commanding position we gazed down on the sweeping countryside where the sun was setting over the mountains which looked ghostly in the evening glow. As darkness fell, a myriad of lights twinkled around the bay below.

Gingerly we climbed down the smooth granite blocks of the path, rounded by the tread of many feet. The whispering zephyrs almost echoed the conversations of antiquity.

In vivid contrast we drove down through the night into the brightly-lit centre of Argos. People were sitting round drinking and chatting; shops overflowing with souvenirs lured the tourist; and attractive postcards added a further note of gaiety. It was difficult to imagine that these may have been the descendants of those who had inhabited the city above.

****

Over the next few days we journeyed northwards along the east coast of Greece. Leaving Athens and its Acropolis to our right, we found that the mountains became higher, and we caught glimpses of the blue Aegean fingering its way between them, and opening into deep bays.

A roadside shrine to an Eastern Orthodox saint

Donkey carts and red-roofed villages became common, while black-frocked old ladies and colourful wayside shrines to saints reminded us of the influence of the Eastern Orthodox church in these regions.

As we approached the town of Katerini, we looked up to the left and saw the great mass of Mount Olympus looming above. It looked both grand and forbidding, and one could imagine the ancient Greeks consigning their gods to live on its uplands.

We stopped briefly for shopping in Thessalonica, named for the daughter of Philip II, the father of Alexander the Great.

One lunchtime, we took a break on the beach of the Gulf of Strimonikos, and after a meal, siesta and swim decided to push on. However, we had underestimated the softness of the sand, and to our consternation the back wheels of the van decided not to propel us forwards, but rather to dig a hole towards Australia. Realising that we were hopelessly stuck, Mike unearthed the snow chains from the locker on the roof, but soon discovered that they were useless in sand.

"Can I be of assistance to you?" boomed a voice from the far end of the beach. Soon a charming, and burly, Greek family was assembled around our vehicle, which with considerable effort was persuaded to rise from its silicon grave.

"Eucharisto! Eucharisto!" was all we could do to express our thanks, but the father of the family replied in excellent English.

"You are most certainly welcome. We always like to help the British. We have not forgotten the war."

Resulting from this delay, we travelled as quickly as possible along the road to Philippi, but dusk came on quite soon, and the twilight drive became quite hair-raising. Unlit donkey carts would suddenly loom up, and deep ditches lined the road, while at the same time the traffic increased heavily. We thought it wise to pull off the road for the night, and found a suitable open space, where we began to prepare for bed. Just as we were turning in, we heard footsteps, and saw the light of a torch coming towards us. We greeted the arrival warily, fearing it was an irate landowner come to kick us off – or, worse still, someone with nefarious intentions. However, it turned out to be a shepherd boy guarding his flock nearby, who wanted to practise his little English from schooldays, and told us he was sixteen and named John. Armed with a box of matches we had given him for cooking his supper, he left us to return to his night vigil.

By this time, we were running along the narrow strip of Greek land between Bulgaria and the Aegean Sea, and bordered on the east by the huge landmass of Turkey. Our departure from Greece would take place at the little town with a big name, Alexandroupolis, and would mark a dramatic cultural shift for us.

Chapter 4
Turkish Delight

From icons to imams, from churches and cathedrals to mosques and minarets - these were some of the changes as we crossed the next frontier. We were leaving the Christian world to enter the sphere of Islam, which had radically influenced the areas through which we were to travel for the next few thousand miles.

Traffic was light at the Greek border post and we passed through quickly, but when we reached the Turkish office, we found that we had been pre-empted by a coach-load of travellers that had just arrived - so it was a slow business. Eventually we were greeted by the customs officer.

"Welcome to Turkey. I hope you will enjoy your stay. How far are you going into our country?"

"Actually we are heading towards India."

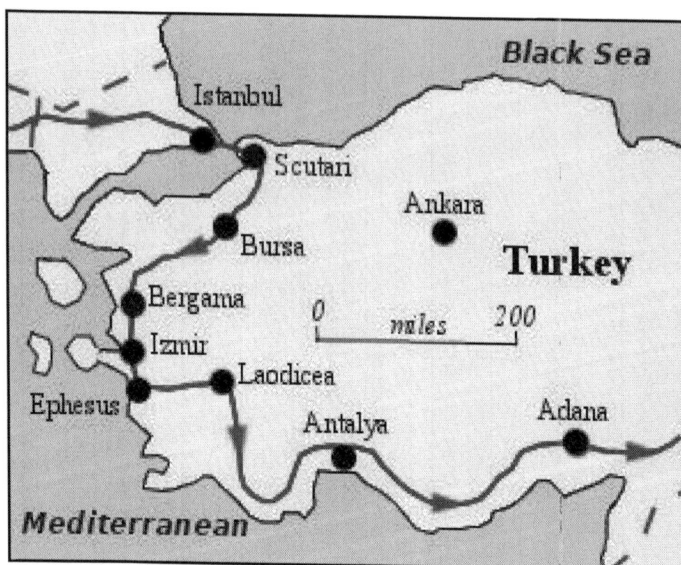

"Oh, that's a long journey. But enjoy our beaches while you can. Once you leave Turkey it will be hot and dry."

With these cheering words we were on our way across European Turkey. Our first impressions of the country were of sandy hills.

A prehistoric-looking lizard dashed across the road, its yellow camouflage useless on the tar surface. We passed acres of sunflowers, whose huge heads all nodded eastwards like Muslims hearing the prayer call.

A major change was the preponderance of mosques, with minarets like rockets pointing vertically into the sky, while the prayer call floated on the still air.

The style of dress began to change too. Women in long blouses, baggy trousers and headscarves left only their faces showing, and many covered themselves completely as we passed. Some of the men were wearing cummerbunds, wide belts tied round their waists, and a few were sporting head-dresses.

The road was very bumpy, although it improved as we neared Istanbul, but at one point had subsided, requiring an extensive diversion. Eventually we pulled into the BP Mocamp with its superb facilities.

****

Next morning we left the campsite to search for a bus which would take us into Istanbul city. Soon one of the minibuses stopped, but was completely full. Undisturbed by this fact, the driver beckoned us aboard, where a small boy whipped out a tiny stool on which I sat. Mike meanwhile was supported upright by the press of bodies all around him. It did not need a linguistics expert to translate the conversation, which centred on this peculiar male who allowed his wife to sit while he stood. What was the world coming to where men deferred to their womenfolk! A study in cultures, indeed!

This sardine tin deposited us near the centre of the metropolis, into a world of blaring horns, raucous street-traders, shoeshine boys, water-sellers and public weighing-machines. We strolled past the university, high on its cliff, as we searched for the Blue Mosque. On finding it, we entered the cool, quiet sanctuary, so named for the predominant colour of its internal decoration. At the entrance I was issued with a blue robe to cover my unsightly knees - although Mike did not concur with this assessment of them. Additionally, we were required to remove our shoes, so that we could pad quietly across the beautiful carpets covering the floor. The building had fluted pillars, painted tiles and an ornate ceiling. There was a high pulpit, but little other furniture apart from a water-tap.

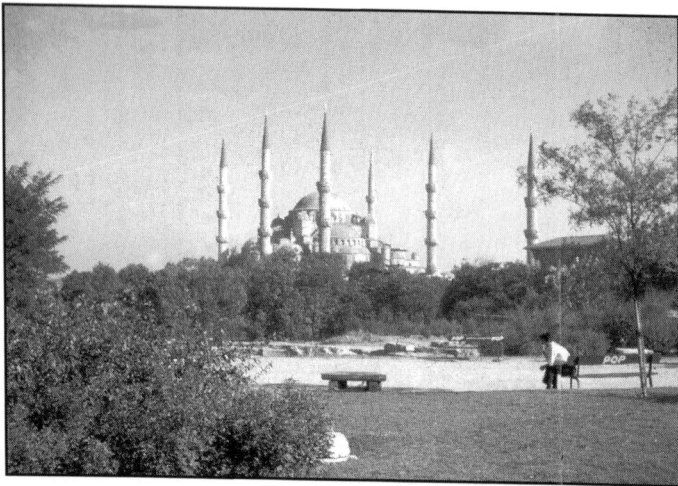

The Blue Mosque in Istanbul

We left the mosque, resisting the little boys selling toys and the men displaying Arabic manuscripts, and wandered down to the harbour. A smell of fish drifted along the quay, and we went to seek its source. A small boat was moored to the dockside, carrying a charcoal brazier on which fresh fish was tantalisingly cooking. Pieces of this, together with hunks of bread, were being passed up to customers on the promenade.

Varieties of transport in Istanbul

Very fresh fish served on the quay

It was with weary feet that we finished our trek through the city, having visited the "souk", the bazaar where almost everything was for sale at a negotiable price.

Insufficient time prevented us from taking a proper look at Hagia Sophia, also known as Sancta Sophia, the Greek Orthodox basilica dating from 500 AD.

Our overwhelming sensation was that Istanbul was a meeting-place. Geographically, it was the bridge between Europe and Asia, as we realised looking across the Bosphorus which we would be crossing the next day. Culturally, it joined the West and the East in terms of traditions and philosophy. Historically, it had been the crux of huge revolutions as it changed from Constantinople to Byzantium to Istanbul, each name denoting the forces pulling at this city from each side.

****

We left Istanbul by queuing up for the Bosphorus ferry. As the heavily-laden vessel ploughed across the short stretch of water, we said farewell to Europe and looked across the bows towards Asia. Ahead lay Scutari, the infamous town where Florence Nightingale nursed soldiers from the Crimean war. We tried to imagine how she must have felt landing on this shore and entering a filthy hospital in a dirty town.

Soon we were out of the twisting streets of the town and following the beautiful coast of the Sea of Marmara.

The filler that Mike had used to seal the radiator repeatedly failed, and as we drove down the west coast of Turkey, we were continually refilling our cooling system. We knew that this problem, which had dogged us for so long, had to be rectified before we moved into the wilder parts of our journey.

Having found a lovely little campsite near Bursa, we decided to visit the top of the Turkish mountain called Uludag, "Sublime Mountain", outside the town. The Greeks had several mountains called Olympus in their empire, and this was one of them. To avoid confusion they called it Mysian Olympus on one side and Bithynian Olympus on the other. So much for reducing confusion! In our heavy hiking boots we clambered aboard a bus that came rolling along, since it appeared to be going in the right direction. As soon as we boarded, a man leapt to his feet and offered his seat, since it is possible that I might have been the only woman ever to use that vehicle. We refused the passengers' pressing offers of cigarettes, and sat smiling knowledgeably as they chattered on in Turkish. The driver declined to accept our fare, and so we climbed out at the funicular station. The cable-car itself was large, taking over forty passengers. We proceeded up the mountain, watching the people relaxing on the grass below, and the town becoming smaller. Following the cable-car stage, we had to transfer to a chair-lift which took us to the summit of Mount Olympus.

The day was very fresh and clear. As we glided over river valleys and across steep slopes, delicate fronds were suspended from the branches of the slender pine trees. Mountain streams plunged their way down into the valley, and the mist swirled around us when we reached the top. Being summer time, there was only a small dirty patch of snow to designate the summit. We stopped in a small restaurant for a drink and saw some plate-sized wafer ice-creams, one of which we tried between us. Perhaps Walls in the U.K. would be interested in taking up the idea! While enjoying our refreshments, we were approached tentatively by a young Turkish lad.

"Please, are you Englishman people?"

"Yes, we come from England. You speak English very well."

"My English is not well, and I have never met Englishmen before."

We invited him to sit with us, and saw how excited he was to have indigenous speakers with whom to practise. We benefited from his local knowledge and life in the region.

"What is your name?"

"I am called Nurettin, and I live in Bursa. I am in the high school now, and want to go to the university in Ankara."

"What would you like to study?"

"I want to be a doctor. Turkey needs many more doctors, but my father wants me to be an engineer. But engineers do not help people in the same way as doctors do."

We chatted with him for quite a while, learning much about the education system in Turkey, which seemed remarkably similar to the British one. When it was time to descend from the chilly summit, Nurettin stuck to us like a limpet - which was just as well, since when we reached the halfway cable station we found it swarming with Turkish families returning from a day out on the mountain. Nurettin carefully steered us through the crowd to a cabin belonging to some friends of his. They invited us into the warmth of their home while we waited for the cable-car queue to diminish. We sat round a wood-burning stove with its glowing ashes, and it was very cosy in the cabin with all the family sitting together, and the wall lined with bottles. The youngest boy of the family was learning English at school, but was too shy to speak, and ran out of the room in embarrassment.

At last we found places in a cable-car to take us down the hill, and after bidding farewell to Nurettin, we returned to our campsite. It was well after midnight when we finally finished a meal and headed into bed.

****

Next morning Mike had to seal the radiator with resin since it was continually leaking because of the high pressure due to the temperatures.

We headed south along the Turkish coast and the rolling hills suddenly changed to pine-forested mountains. Many of the trees had V-shaped cuts in the bark under which little cups were tied to catch the resin - obviously part of some local industry.

Collecting pine resin

Running water - if you pump!

The radiator blew a hole as we climbed the mountain road so we decided to stop by the roadside at a water supply, and I began to prepare a meal of sardines and rice. As I opened the tin, a revoltingly foul smell of drains assailed our nostrils. Without delay, Mike picked the offending object and flung it as far as he could into the bush below. In consequence we decided to open one of our remaining packs of bacon and enjoy an English meal. Our lunch was accompanied by the voice of the muezzin, floating across to us from the mosque in the valley nearby.

We decided to stop at the next town of any size and look for someone to fix the radiator problem. Soon we reached a small settlement in which we found a tinsmith tucked away in the back streets, and who seemed competent for the job. By vivid gesticulations, we indicated that our radiator needed to be made watertight again. The mechanic did not seem at all surprised at this, and we concluded that in summertime Turkey many vehicles suffered from this ailment. It soon became obvious that the man had done this before, and after half an hour with a hot soldering iron, he indicated that the job was done. He also showed us by graphic demonstration that we should continue our journey with the radiator filler-cap only turned loosely on the top. At first Mike was suspicious of this, since the pressurised water system would not function, but after following his advice we discovered that he was right. It meant that we needed to top up more frequently, but at least the radiator did not burst again.

Having paid the artisan, we climbed into the van and drove back up the street of the town. Suddenly there was a great commotion! We heard a whistle being blown and shouts behind us. On stopping, we were surrounded by a crowd - all keen to give us some important information. Out of the mass stepped a uniformed person, who was clearly a policeman. Despite the language barrier, it was obvious that he was berating us about something. Eventually, while we looked nonplussed, he took Mike by the arm and marched him down the road, pointing out a sign which unequivocally declared that this was a one-way street - and that our way was not the one-way. Looking as penitent as possible, we indicated our chagrin at having contravened the laws of Turkey. At first we suspected he was looking for a bribe, but after a while his face relaxed and he waved us on our way - making certain that we were travelling in the right direction along the street!

That night, while sleeping in the van, I was awakened by a bright light shining on my face. I sat up, startled for a moment. There were gaps in the curtains and a torch moved from one to the next round the camper, accompanied by a muttering. After a while the light disappeared, and the observer went away.

****

As we headed south we drove into the town of Bergama, above which we saw the ruins of the ancient city of Pergamum. The road wound its way up the hill, but unlike other ancient cities, it had a good surface. The historical site was more commercialised than most, and postcards and pottery were on sale. Having paid the entrance fee, we climbed up into the old city with a guide book written in quaint English. It was very hot exploring the ruins, but we soon forgot the blazing sun as we imagined life in this enormous city which had been the focal point of a powerful kingdom over 2000 years ago. Eventually the city fathers donated their kingdom to the Romans to prevent a civil war. The Greek gods were worshipped here, and a grand altar to Zeus had been established in the main temple. Being such a centre of paganism, it was not surprising that early Christians called it "Satan's seat". We clambered through the ancient streets and marvelled at the impressive architecture as well as the magnificent view of the Aegean coast.

Exploring the ruins of Pergamum, "Satan's Seat"

After leaving Pergamum, we drove down the coastal road until we found an access point to the sea, whereupon we plunged our hot bodies into the cool Mediterranean, and were greatly refreshed.

****

Our route took us on through Turkey's third largest city, Izmir formerly known as Smyrna. We gazed at its sweeping natural harbour with a renowned ship-building industry, and then journeyed up the Hermas valley. As we did so, the heat became oppressive, and we could see a storm brewing up on the mountains around. Being late afternoon, we took the opportunity to stop for a meal at a wayside motel which was offering shish kebab and salad. As the wind became stronger, the waiters ran around shutting doors and windows, while fork and sheet lightning flashed on the mountains bordering the valley. The weather on all sides was menacing, but we were right in the middle of the storm and escaped the really heavy rain. And so we enjoyed our Turkish evening repast.

One feature of Turkish life was the endless succession of "chai" shops in every town and village. They served small cups of tea, and provided a centre for the men to meet, talk, sleep and drink tea. I suppose they were the equivalent of the pub in English culture. But, being a Muslim country, tea was the strongest drink that was consumed.

However, we never saw a woman in a chai shop. In fact, one morning as we drove through the Turkish villages, I realised that I was the only woman around at that time of day. It seemed that women never sat in the tea shops, and rarely appeared outside fields or houses. I was thankful that I was not born a Turkish woman, and I wished I could lead an emancipation campaign - and give these men who sat about all day something positive to think about and do. Shades of my former political activism appearing again!

On one occasion we stopped on the road for breakfast in the van, and a farm worker came over to talk and then disappeared. A few minutes later he re-emerged with an armful of grapes. He left us again and then returned accompanied by three friends each with another armful! Four children were with them, who pressed us for a photograph to be taken, after which they wrote down names and addresses for copies to be sent to them. I did wonder where Mum was! We left that spot with a bucket of grapes on the roof.

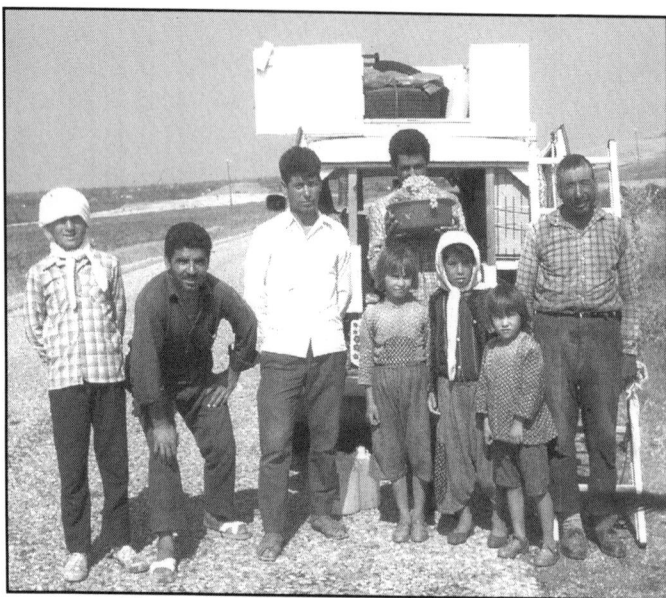

The generous grape-giving Turkish family

****

Not long afterwards, the van hit an enormous rut in the road at about 40 mph and we feared for the state of the undercarriage. After a sweaty investigation underneath, Mike concluded that no serious harm had been done.

We were really longing to see the ancient city of Sardis, once the capital of the fabulous empire of Lydia which during the sixth and fifth centuries B.C. had dominated an area almost the same as modern Turkey. Imagine our surprise and disappointment when we discovered that all that remained of this capital was a corner of stonework on the peak of a high hill.

All that remained of proud Sardis

Nevertheless, we wanted to reach the top and felt certain the view would be worth the effort. But we looked in vain for a way up the craggy hillside. Suddenly there was a shout, and two little figures detached themselves from a herd of cows grazing nearby. Then we saw two tiny girls running towards us waving frantically. With smiles and chatter they greeted us, and so we took the opportunity to converse with them in sign language.

"Which is the way to the top of the mountain?" we asked with fluent finger pointing.

They replied with enthusiastic body language indicating a route, and then grasped our hands and began to lead us up the hill. It was much steeper than it had looked from the base, and before long we were climbing on a narrow pathway through steep rocks.

The agile sisters

Our two guides were so nimble that we suspected a check of their chromosomes would have revealed a large dose of mountain-goat DNA. Running ahead, almost vertically, they would wait for us with broad grins as we panted up. Half an hour later we were nearing the top and the narrow path suddenly came to an end. A rock fall had removed a section of about three metres from the path and deposited it in the valley 2000 feet below. All that remained on the rock face was a narrow ledge about 20 cm wide which was obviously impossible to cross. But it appeared that the Turkish language did not contain the word "impossible" - certainly for agile Turkish girls. Without pausing, they skipped along the narrow shelf to safety on the far side where the path continued. Next moment they were back, seizing our hands and pulling us across this terrifying abyss where we dared not look down. From there we continued to the rocky top where the corner of a stone wall was the only evidence of the city's former strength. We saw the most amazing view up the valley to the mountains of inland Turkey.

The hills of inland Turkey from the summit of ruined Sardis

One of the little girls ran along a narrow ridge with a steep drop on either side, looked down at her cows grazing below, and noticed something was wrong. She skipped back to us, and with a quick wave the two little maidens ran swiftly back along the ledge and down the mountain, leaving us isolated on the summit.

It did not take long for us to reach a consensus that we wanted to find an alternative way down. We were doubtful that we could survive the ledge along the abyss without ending up in the valley below as corpses. In vain we searched for another route, but the thick prickly pear vegetation blocked our way. Regretfully, with our hearts in our mouths, we negotiated the terrifying section, and made our way down.

****

Our next objective was the famous city of Ephesus, the Greek jewel beside the Mediterranean. We found a campsite on the beach near to the ancient site and, after giving a motorist a tow out of the sand, we changed for a welcome swim. As evening fell, we spotted a wooden building half over the sea supported on stilts. Our guess that this was a restaurant proved right, and so instead of digging into our meagre food supply, we went to have a look. The proprietor showed us into a little kitchen, in the usual fashion, where we peered into the various pots on the stove to make our orders. Some small flat fish looked interesting, and so we indicated we would have some. Sitting on the balcony watching the sunset, we awaited our meal. When it came, it turned out that the fish were not filleted or beheaded, but the taste was good. However, as we struggled with a myriad of tiny bones, the sun finally vanished and the electricity supply became progressively weaker until we could not discern the food on our plates. The manager rushed up with a small candle, and apologised in Turkish for the illumination failure - at least we assumed that was what he was doing. The remainder of the meal was undertaken in almost pitch darkness with a flickering flame, as we picked out tiny bones with our fingers. It was an interesting tactile experience, and gave new meaning to the term "candle-lit dinner".

Next morning we made an early start, and after a quick cup of tea, we arrived at the entrance to the historic city at 6.15 am while it was still cool. To our disappointment, we discovered that the gate to the city did not open until 8 o'clock. So we took the opportunity to have a leisurely and sumptuous breakfast in the car park. Promptly at opening time, we entered the city before anyone else - and soon

- 46 -

realised that this was the most comprehensive ruined city we had so far explored on our journey.

As we walked along the Arcadian Way, we found it hard to believe that the city had existed for 3000 years. This main boulevard ran for half a mile from the ancient harbour through to the great theatre and city centre of Ephesus. In its day this roadway was colonnaded along its length with shops and restaurants on either side. During the Roman period it had street lamps at night, being only one of three cities in the Empire with such luxury. We visualised the bustling busyness that must have existed in those days, as merchants hurried to the harbour to meet ships, toga-clad matrons wandered through the shops, slaves carrying loads plodded by, and children played games on the marble slabs of the roadway. Visiting dignitaries were welcomed by elaborate ceremonies and grand displays along the roadway as they made their way into the main city. We could picture Agamemnon being carried in his litter through the colonnade to be greeted by the city's elders.

The Arcadian Way with the remains of its colonnade

We were told that the harbour on the River Cayester had silted up over the centuries, and the sea had retreated about five miles. The shops had completely disappeared, although many of the stately columns still lined the thoroughfare.

On arrival at the amphitheatre, we were amazed at the size and condition of it. Seating 25,000 people, it was arranged with a large stage in three tiers. The temperature rose rapidly as we climbed up the steps to the main theatre. As an experiment, Mike stood in the middle of the podium and made a Socratic-type speech to the whole audience gathered there. It was actually only me, and I had heard it before! We were astonished that without great effort his voice could carry to the top rows of the seating. Those Greeks had no need of PA systems!

The Ephesian theatre

Mike acting the orator

We wandered up the ancient streets, and discovered many Greek inscriptions on the walls of the amazing buildings which filled this ancient metropolis.

****

Driving on from Ephesus, we passed olive groves, orchards of fig trees, fields of melons, and dried-up river beds, as we travelled through sandy coloured mountains. We passed the yellow Meander River, which lived up to its circuitous name. A group of camels was resting under a tree in the heat of the day, no doubt for their drivers benefit and not for them.

A long, slow climb up through the mountains took us to the ruins of Pammukale, where some quite spectacular limestone formations were to be seen. The calcium-laden hot water coming out of the hills around had produced protrusions like great icicles suspended over waterfalls and shallow pools. We paddled in the warm water, and climbed up to watch the steaming spring water rushing down to the valley below. We stared across the vista, trying to work out where our next destination would be.

Paddling in hot lime-laden waters

Hot water from Pammukale rushing into the valley

For years we had been fascinated by a little town in western Turkey called Laodicea which, together with Pergamum, Sardis and Ephesus, figured in the book of Revelation in the Bible. Apparently it was unusual, because in antiquity its water supply produced lukewarm water, which was used for certain types of textile processing. The reason was that the hot spring water from Pammukale was piped for several miles into Laodicea, arriving at a tepid temperature. As we headed down the valley and into its environs, it soon became obvious that there were no helpful road-signs, and we believed that the town was not inhabited. Quite a challenge! So we took to asking people along the road, but we only knew the town by its Greek name, Laodicea, and everyone looked blank when we mentioned it. Starting below the hot springs and following little trails we searched the valley without success. Rather despondently we rejoined the main road, and again made inquiries there. Suddenly we saw beside the road a small boy holding up pottery.

"Antique! Antique!" he shouted. But we took no notice, having encountered many other youngsters touting fake relics in these regions.

"Antique - from Laodicea," he repeated loudly.

The helpful boy who, with his friends, revealed the lost city

With great gusto I slammed on the brakes, causing the van to skid through the dust for a while. The little boy came running up expectantly.

"You want antiques? Nice antiques!"

"No thanks. But do you know Laodicea?"

"I know. I go with you."

We could not believe that he definitely knew the name of the town, but we were ready to follow any lead. He jumped aboard and directed us down a long, stony, road towards some distant ruins in a side valley.

As we rounded a bend on the hillside we saw a huge open area littered with stone blocks and pottery fragments. This was certainly an ancient town, but was it Laodicea? As we walked through the dusty fields, the little boy showed us a carving of a young boy, a Christian cross incised on a block, and the remains of two large amphitheatres.

However, there was no sign of the rumoured water-pipes for which we were looking. We tried to convey the idea to the boy, but to no avail. At last we turned and made our way back towards the van.

Ruins at Laodicea

Suddenly I stumbled over a half-buried stone, and noticed it had a hole through it. Looking around, we saw more prominent ones scattered around the area, each almost a one metre cube with a central 15 cm hole between the faces. On one side was a lip and on the other a chamfer, suggesting that these blocks were intended to fit together as a continuous pipe. The inside of the hole had a thick deposit of limestone. Without doubt, this was part of an ancient pipeline.

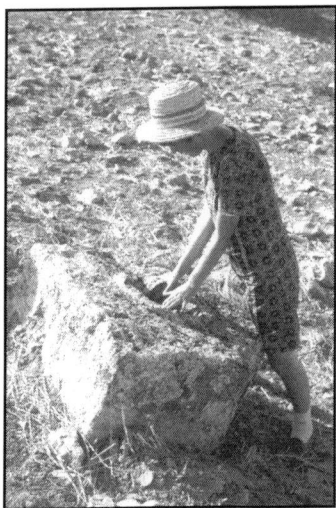

The carefully sculptured block

I was sure that the boy had never seen people so excited by a stone before, but then he realised it was important and ran back to the road. Soon he was joined by other youngsters. As we came out of the ruins the group motioned to us to go up the hill, and there we discovered a long line of these stones stretching down the hillside, to provide a continuous watercourse supplying the ancient city.

By this time, half the nearby villagers were out to see these peculiar foreigners. A large group of children followed Mike as he investigated the pipeline high up on the hill, and he concluded that this was the supply route that brought water from the hot springs that we had seen earlier in the day. The children showed great interest in his investigations, and when he came down the slope he looked like the Pied Piper of Hamelin.

The amazing stone pipeline that carried hot water to Laodicea

****

One afternoon, as we drove further through the countryside of southern Turkey, we came upon a real Constable scene. Threshing and winnowing were in progress. Wooden sledges were being pulled across the corn by horses or oxen. Other people were throwing the grain in the air to separate it from the chaff. We really wondered if we had stepped back in time and place to 18th Century England - to somewhere far from the madding crowd. One could imagine Thomas Hardy sitting on the hillside writing his stories.

Recent days had taken us inland towards the centre of Turkey, but now we turned back towards the coast again. After crossing an impressive mountain range, we drove down towards the blue sea. Passing through a freshwater marsh area where water lilies opened their petals to take the sun, and through pinewood slopes flanking the road, we arrived in Attalia - and headed for the beach. By this time the temperature in the van was nearly 40°C as we arrived at a beautiful sandy bay called Lara Plaji. We had cups of chai at a small stall, and then in the heat Mike foolishly accepted a glass of cold water to go with the tea. Within a few hours the bugs in the water had turned his stomach into a painful bacterial battleground.

That night we hunted for a suitable camping place until quite late, and then spotted a sign to a site. We drove down a narrow lane for about three miles, and found a beautiful location in a pine forest. In view of the ethereal environment and the high temperature, we decided to sleep on the roof. It was certainly a lovely experience, with a few stars twinkling above us through the leafy roof. Next morning we walked through the woodland to find the sea, breathing in the deeply pine-scented air.

On another afternoon we spied a beautiful beach and turned off the road to try and cool down in the inviting water. Donning goggles and flippers we managed to swim out to an offshore rock, narrowly missing some sharp pieces of granite protruding from the sea-bed. Below the surface we found some wonderful rock formations and marine life. However, our privacy was short-lived, as a contingent of Turkish teenagers who had spotted us decided to swim out to join the fun. They were mischievous youngsters, who seemed bent on trying to be a nuisance to us. So, using the advantage of wearing flippers, we managed to outdistance them easily, and returned to the beach. Then the group of lively boys followed us, and soon made life difficult. Thus we packed up, and moved on to a quieter spot.

****

After these weeks of constant traveling, we were looking forward to a quiet weekend at a large well-advertised campsite at Silifke. Thinking that we were almost at the camp, we conjured up in our minds the delicious meal which we anticipated in the camp restaurant. However, it transpired that the Mocamp was at the foot of the mountains 30 miles east of the town through which we had to pass.

As we drove along the main street, we found it was thronged with people, and threading our way through the mass of humanity, we could see flames ahead of us. A policeman motioned us to keep our distance, and we found that we were crawling behind a student procession armed with flaming torches and banners. Inviting smells floated from roadside restaurants, but we were anxious to reach the camp and so did not stop. At last, our destination came in sight and we enjoyed its excellent facilities for the weekend – swimming, resting, reading, writing and eating. Mike was still suffering from the tummy bug resulting from his unwise drink, but he knew it was time to grease and check the van thoroughly. Despite his condition, he endured this activity in the great heat, while I did a mass of washing, as well as a cleanout of the van.

We knew we were about to cross the Rubicon. This was the last sight of the sea that we would have for many weeks - in fact until reaching the Indian ocean. From now on, it would be dry hills, high temperatures - and dust, dust and more dust. The days of golden beaches and blue-water swimming were past, and we did not expect to see an ocean for many a steaming mile.

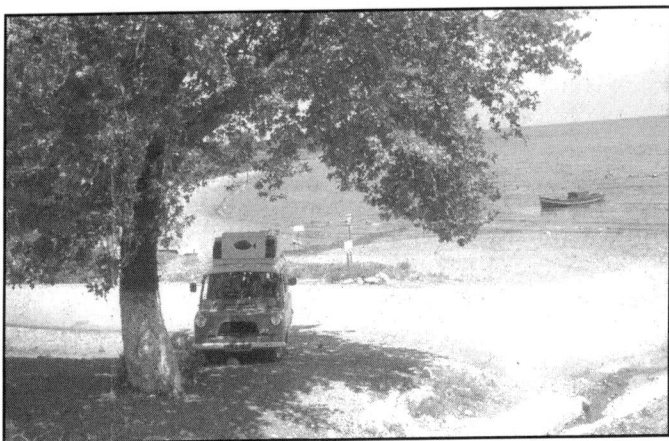

Our final experience of Turkish beaches

By this time we had covered the major part of Turkey, but there still remained the need to cross the eastern half of the country, which was reportedly much wilder and more of a challenge for route-finding. We knew that a new page of our journey was about to begin.

Our experience of Turkey to this point had truly been a delight - but now we would be heading north-east towards central Asia.

Chapter 5
Approaching Ararat

Although there was reputedly a good road through the north of Turkey, we decided to venture into the south-eastern part of the country instead, and then rejoin the main road near to the crossing into Iran. Reports suggested that this would be a wild area of poor roads and poorer people, and we expected to be oddities on the landscape in our western vehicle and dress.

Having passed through Tarsus, a bustling and joyous little town, once the home of Paul the apostle, we drove into the large city of Adana, and then out into the russet hills beyond.

The surface deteriorated as the road climbed into the mountains, but the scenery was terrific with huge craggy ranges stretching into the distance. At the roadside were small villages and clusters of tents protected with branches against the sun and wind.

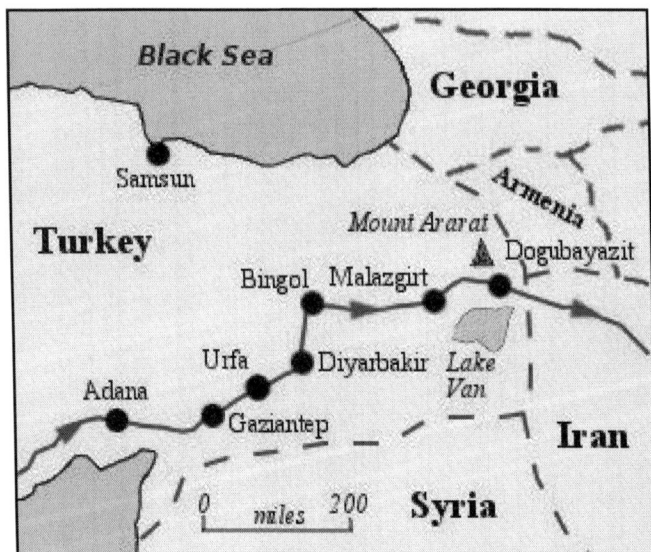

Cows and goats grazed dreamily on the sparse grassy patches. Bulging hand-woven sacks were piled by the roadside awaiting collection.

We stopped at the top of a pass, and gazed down into a valley about thirty miles wide stretching all the way into Syria. All we could see of that ancient land were low desertified hills right to the horizon. Straining our eyes, we searched for Gaziantep, our next port of call, and eventually perceived it nestling in the valley 2000 feet below us. Descending the long hairpins of the rough road, we found ourselves in a white-walled Arab city quite unlike any we had seen before.

Looking into Syria from Turkey with Gaziantep in the valley

To our surprise, we found that we could purchase ice in these remote places, and in view of the extreme heat and the fact that the Turkish lira had just been devalued by 25%, we celebrated by buying an icebox at a little stall on the muddy main road of Gaziantep. Since cans of drink seemed to be ubiquitous in central Asia, this purchase ensured a source of refreshment as we moved into hotter regions.

****

Leaving the town, our route took us through sandy, rocky countryside. Coming down a hill, we were awed to see a majestic eagle perched motionless on a telegraph pole silhouetted against the evening sky.

By this time, campsites had become a thing of the past, and for the future we planned to stop at night near to habitation wherever possible. Certainly, we would try to avoid camping in very isolated places, but our policy did not always work out. It occurred to us that we might find security in parking at police posts or petrol stations.

We found one of the latter just outside the town of Urfa, and were welcomed by a young student who was helping man the pumps there. He spoke a little English and Mike accepted his invitation for chai. The student then pressed us to try a special concoction called "iran", an odiforous, thinned yogurt drink. Unwillingly, Mike accepted a glass, watched intently by our host, and bravely consumed this unappetising draught. Sadly Mike forgot the Arab custom of saying "No more, thank you" by rubbing the glass between the fingers.

"You like, yes? Very good, yes."

"Well, er, very nice - but that will be suff..."

The result was an immediate refill, which Mike managed to drink down in one gulp - followed by so much rubbing of the glass that it nearly cracked. The kind student then insisted on filling several bottles with this liquid for our onward journey. The smell and taste of this delicacy was like extremely sour, putrid milk, and so we quietly treated the bushes to a long drink. We spent the night at the filling station, and enjoyed our time conversing with the young man. He was quite surprised when we asked where to throw our rubbish - it seemed to him quite obvious. When we saw the litter disfiguring the valley below, we understood.

****

Still the road continued to climb into the mountains of eastern Turkey. Mike was still feeling queasy from his foolish drink at Lara Plaji, plus the recent encounter with "iran". He had frequent bouts of sickness, and so slept on the bunk in the back of the van - which left me to do the driving. At one point, as we approached a police roadblock, the officer's eyes popped right out of his head. A lone woman driving an empty van was more than he had ever seen before! He seemed quite mesmerised by my presence at the steering wheel, and so with a broad, and slightly salacious, grin he waved me on. As the vehicle slid slowly past him, Mike arose from his couch in the back, and waved genially to the man. His face would have made a marvellous picture if we had happened to have the camera handy.

It was now my turn to experience a stomach bug, and so I stayed on the bunk in the back while Mike did the driving. Unfortunately he did not impress the local constabulary as much as I did. Nevertheless we made steady, if not rapid, progress across the ranges.

The mighty Euphrates River during the dry season

At one point we came over a hill and saw ahead a whitewashed town of considerable size on the far bank of a broad river. A quick consultation of the map confirmed that we were about to cross the famous Euphrates, even though in mid-summer it was shallow and sandy, with some agriculture on the flood-plain.

Bit by bit we climbed up to a plain, and then through undulating hills, heading for Diyarbakir. About twenty miles from the town we suddenly heard a loud rattling sound as though a huge lorry were overtaking us. A quick check in the mirror showed no vehicle in sight. Stopping quickly, an investigation revealed the silencer trailing along the ground under the vehicle, barely attached to the exhaust pipe. Mike wrestled with the hot metal for a while, finally managing to disengage the silencer and stow it on the roof. As we restarted, a noise like a motorbike accompanied us.

****

A Common Defense Early Warning Station with huge aerials pointing north-east reminded us of our Russian neighbours. This spot was the only area of flattish land before the border, since huge ranges of mountains lay between Russia and this point. A convoy of more than fifty jeeps and lorries heading for the Diyarbakir army base, after an exercise, was a further reminder of the enmity between the West and the Communist world.

We found Diyarbakir to be an old-established and very busy town. Sensing the sound and smell coming from our van, the residents were not slow in directing us to the central repair area. "Exhaust" was the word on their lips when we stopped to inquire the way. We found a superb area with many small businesses. A chair was immediately produced for me, and they began the job on the exhaust system without delay. The area was well equipped with modern tools and oxy-acetylene equipment. The mechanic found a silencer, but it was the wrong size and so he deftly made a piece of pipe to weld onto our silencer at one end and then to the remains of our exhaust pipe at the other. It was fascinating to watch his delicate work on the anvil. He made some metal straps to hold the system in place under the vehicle. There were several small boys about eight years old running around with tools. Meanwhile, in an adjacent part of the yard, another chap removed a nail from a tyre and mended a puncture for us. A farmer overseeing a tractor repair supplied us with chai and cokes - and a table and stools appeared from the friendly mechanics.

****

We left Diyarbakir in the late afternoon, and dusk came upon us quite quickly. Soon the evening stars appeared and shone brightly above us. The road deteriorated to poor quality stabilised gravel - in some cases quite unstabilised. We hurried on, hoping to reach the next town where we could spend the night. As the roadway became a mixture of sand and pebbles the van's lights flickered madly. Then, after a mile of this, the engine cut out completely, leaving us on a bend of the road in complete darkness. It was obviously an ignition fault caused by the constant vibration. However, we did not have much chance to feel lonely. Within a short time, six lorries stopped to help. Turkish drivers felt around in the engine compartment with loud arguments about the diagnosis, despite Mike's exhortation to "Please leave it alone!" One excited fellow had a little English mixed up with French.

"Please, Monsieur, let me repair your problem."

"I think I can manage, thank you."

"Je sais this is an injury electronique. I will heal it."

This gentleman was so persistent that I unplugged the inspection lamp, to prevent him and friends from wrecking our engine. Howls of despair arose when the light went out. Unperturbed by this development, and very indignant, our bilingual friend waltzed around to the back of the van and tried to take out our gas lamp to balance on top of the engine. At one stage ten voluble fellows were intent on helping us. So we decided it was time to have a meal, and indicated that the restorative operation was in abeyance for a while. At this, they waved cheerily, climbed into their lorries, and rumbled away. Only one remained, being a young guy who apparently lived nearby, and so we gave him tea while we ate. Finally we made it into bed at 1 am, having left a warning triangle in the road behind us.

Site of the encounter with the "helpful" Turkish drivers

The next morning Mike started work on the engine at 6 am, and with the advantage of daylight he found the fault fairly soon. It was a cable connection to the coil, dislodged by the vibrations of the rough road. Before long, the vehicle was ticking over once again, and we were on the move. The road surface continued to be very bad until Lake Hazor, where we stopped for a swim and a wash. Another student chose to air his knowledge of English by chatting with us in the beach cafe by the lake.

In the next town, I discovered fresh meat in a refrigerator, together with cheese. I also found a large quantity of ice, an important commodity in this tremendous heat. The shops were fairly well equipped, but difficult to find.

****

The next stretch of road would take us to the town of Bingol. We crossed the Murat River, where cattle were drinking at the water's edge, and the bright sun caused a golden glow making the water sparkle. After the bridge the road deteriorated to poor quality asphalt with 10 cm holes in some places. At one point the thoroughfare had subsided completely, and there was a tricky diversion. Rocky outcrops were visible among the mountains but little cultivation, and consequently a very low population in the area. The villages were clusters of stone houses with rough mortar and corrugated iron roofs.

As darkness fell we neared Bingol. There had been no petrol stations for 80 miles, but we had a good supply on the roof. At one point, I nearly drove into a cow which jumped in front of the van. On arrival in the town centre, we stopped to look for ice in the warm evening. Hordes of boys crowded around the van, and one of them spoke a little English. I refused the invitation to nurse baby Aida, who was being passed from one boy to another. It was quite a small town and the search for ice proved fruitless. In the end we parked for the night at a garage run by two men, who acquiesced happily to us using their forecourt. One of the chaps we nicknamed Bristley, being short, stocky and sporting a week-old beard. His partner became the "Young Chap" in view of his youthful look. Bristley strutted around excitedly with a broad grin on his face, proudly showing us off to all the drivers requiring fuel. The YC, however, hovered near us most of the time we were there, and was fascinated by every move we made in our sleeping bags on the roof. Despite this observation, we had a very comfortable night up top, since it was cool with a light wind blowing.

One noticeable absence in Turkish towns is any sign saying "Toilet". To some extent this may be explained by the fact that these facilities have a pungent method of making their location widely known, but this also severely dissuades one from venturing near the source of the stench. On this particular occasion we were relieved to find that a small copse was situated behind Bristley's garage, providing a welcome alternative to his typically Turkish loo.

****

Next morning, Mike changed the tyres to the heavy-duty "Town and Country" ones that we had been carrying on the roof. These had a very deep tread, rather like tractor tyres, and had been recommended for the more unstable road surfaces. After saying farewell to our good friends at the garage, we headed north out of the town.

A vista of remoteness and isolation in eastern Turkey

The surface deteriorated again to very unstable gravel. We passed a jeep by the roadside with a broken steering track rod, which was not an encouraging sight for us.

"Time for tea!" Mike suddenly announced grimly.

"What d'you mean?" I asked, lifting my eyes from the road as I tried to steer a straight course through the gullies.

"Just listen!"

Then I realised that there was a distinct sound of bubbling water and hissing - not unlike an electric kettle. Pulling onto a fairly level patch beside the road, I watched Mike peer under the bonnet, with sweat streaming down his face.

"Looks like a heater hose has split."

"Do we have any spares?"

"Not of that size. Could be a problem."

Standing in the blazing sun, I remarked casually "Do we really need a heater on this trip?"

"Actually you're right. Maybe I could use the other hose to bypass the heater. Let's try!"

Half an hour later, this suggestion turned into reality, and we had no more trouble on that score.

After a while, the road became narrow and very bumpy. At one point the van was sitting straddled across a boulder and we had to reverse off. In places, rocks had rolled down the mountain and formed a ridge along the centre of the road. Periodically we had to balance the van's wheels on this ridge and the side of the road. A horse shied away from us, obviously unused to motor vehicles. We now realised why sensible people preferred the main road through the north of Turkey!

As though we did not have enough to contend with, we suddenly discovered that the van would not go into second gear. Stopping yet again in the midday sun, Mike probed around the gearbox, and found that a spring had broken.

So yet another jury rig was utilised, as he improvised with a piece of elastic which seemed to solve the problem.

The "main" artery leading to Malazgirt

****

We rounded a bend, and seeing a beautiful concrete bridge ahead, we realised that there must have been plans to rebuild that road sometime in the past. After this, the going improved slightly, and we drove through a fertile area where large well-fed herds were returning from pasture and little villages nestled at the foot of the hillsides. A line of ducks and ducklings exited from a pool of water, and waddled along the edge. A gaggle of geese started to cross the road, saw us, and with one accord marched back again. We pulled into a filling station, but the single pump was empty, although turkeys strutted about as though they owned the place. The corn had been harvested and piles of golden straw lay by the rectangular mud brick houses. A tortoise moved slowly across the road, while electric-blue and green birds with flat heads and pointed beaks darted to and fro.

Our lips were cracked and dry, our noses blocked and lungs full of the ubiquitous yellow dust. But we felt a certain sense of achievement when we drove into Malazgirt, a small remote town in the vastness of the countryside. We located the Jandarma, and were permitted to camp in front of the main office which was an impressive building in the middle of town. As we left to explore the town, the chief of police indicated he would take charge of our vehicle, gun at the ready. We strolled into the main street for a meal of "uscara", a delicious combination of skewered rissoles, tomatoes, onions and bread.

As we sat in the open-air café, enjoying the break from dusty, rough roadways, an elderly man began to chat in quite reasonable English.

"So - where have you come from now?"

"Today we came from Bingol - but before that from Adana and Gaziantep."

"That last part of the road is real bad. Have any problems?"

"Plenty! It was so uneven and unpredictable. We're surprised there was so little traffic."

The man laughed. "Many of the supplies for this town come in by helicopter. Very few people use that road."

Our attention was suddenly diverted by the sight of groups of excited little boys lining the side of the street - all looking expectantly for something to arrive. Then with a ringing of bells, a large red fire-engine came along. It was the standard British Dennis machine with which we were so familiar.

"How on earth did that get here?" I mused.

"Must be a fire somewhere," observed Mike naively.

"No fire. It's the dust," replied our informant.

Looking carefully, we observed that the vehicle had a spraying system mounted on each side, and that the purpose was to damp down the dust that abounded everywhere. It appeared to be a nightly performance, and the youngsters ran alongside enjoying a free cooling shower.

We returned to our vehicle followed by a considerable crowd of curious hangers-on. Outside the Jandarma a policeman had been allocated the task of guarding us for the night. He was so insistently helpful that we utilised him in banging out the dust from our bedding. Turning-in was a very public affair, with police and the general populace watching our every move.

****

Next morning we left at 6.10 am, before the local inhabitants had turned out in sufficient numbers to make us a spectacle. The road was stabilised gravel but had an alarming ridged effect, which jarred and shook the van. This vibration was so severe that before long one front bumper bracket sheared off. So we endured another enforced respite from driving for half an hour, while Mike detached the offending bumper, and stowed it on the roof.

Soon after this, the bolts holding the horn rattled loose, causing the electrical connections to short together whenever we hit a bump. This resulted in a concert of loud hoots, the intensity of which indicated the state of the road. For a while this kept us amused, but when we tired of the sound, Mike produced a spanner and made the horn behave itself.

There were more villages in this area, and women walked along the road in brightly-coloured dresses. Several men were making bricks of mud, ready to bake in the hot sun. Camels were grazing on the stony scrubland behind the houses.

Bumpy roads destroyed bumpers

****

At last we turned onto the main road through northern Turkey and were relieved to be free of the vibration, dust and uncertainty of the last several hundred miles. The asphalt was smooth, although pitted with some small holes. The view was enchanting - low mountains of pink, green and orange with craggy peaks rising behind them. On the fertile grasslands were Bedouin encampments and huge herds.

With a considerable feeling of success, we entered Dogubayazit, the last town before the border with Iran. We were delighted to find a motel rising among the mud-faced, mud-bricked dwellings. Apart from the typical Turkish loo, the place was clean, and we had a delightful room looking up at the majesty of Mount Ararat. There was the inevitable crowd of small boys, watching intently as we unpacked essentials from our dusty vehicle.

We soon found ourselves tucking into shish-kebab in the motel restaurant, and relishing the relative luxury of the place.

View of Ararat from our motel room

Mike recounted the story, and not for the first time, of his idea during student days of an expedition to this region. In the 1960s there were rumours flying around of sightings of a great structure in the ice of Ararat, which some believed was Noah's Ark. Although giving little credence to this theory, Mike and his fellows saw it as a good excuse to propose the Cambridge Ararat Arkeological Expedition, and were hopeful of attracting sponsorship for it. Planning started for a party in two land rovers to travel overland and climb the peak. However, when the Turkish authorities were approached, it transpired that the Ararat region was at that period a sealed military area, where foreigners were not welcome. Thus the grand idea fizzled!

Relaxing in our room with a view, we saw a cloud settle over Ararat, and remain until the late afternoon when it suddenly lifted. The sunset gave the snow a tinge of pink, while the mountain loomed darkly behind, against a pale grey evening sky. Then the snow turned pure white, looking like an awe-inspiring vanilla ice-cream in the fading light.

My sketch of Ararat

On returning from a brief walk in the dusk, we found a group of climbers in the motel vestibule.

"Have you been up the mountain?" we enquired eagerly.

"Yes, this was our first day up there," replied the leader, whose accent betrayed his south London origin. "We've come from a climbing club in the U.K. - and hope to reach the summit."

"And what's it like up there?"

"Not nice at all. There's an icy wind blowing over the ridge. Comes from Russia. And the snow is deep and powdery."

"Surprising - since it's mid-summer," Mike observed.

"Not really. The major peak is nearly 17,000 feet. We only made it to about 12,000 feet today. But we will try again."

"What will it be like further up?"

"Well, since it's a dormant volcano with two peaks, there's a lava flow between the two - and that's now a treacherous ice-field."

We wished them well, and left them to rest and warm up after their ordeal. Consequently, we gazed at the mountain with renewed respect.

Feeling refreshed after a day's rest, we cleaned out the van, watched of course by numerous people. We were learning that the concept of privacy is largely unknown in the east. A tiny kitten played hide-and-seek among our cushions.

The road to the frontier, ten miles away, appeared to be poor quality asphalt. We were apprehensive about what lay on the other side, as we stared at forbidding-looking mountains blocking the way into Iran.

Chapter 6
Persian Carpet

"Iran welcomes the noble visitors. We hope your stay is comfortable and congenial," the immigration officer intoned, in what was obviously a standard formula greeting. He smiled at Mike, who stood with his pile of documents.

The formalities for leaving Turkey had been finished quickly, and now we were parked at the Iranian border. I stayed in the van, while Mike went to deal with officialdom.

"Please may I see your passports, driving licences, registration book and carnet."

Mike was slightly surprised at the last request, since no other country on the route so far had requested that document.

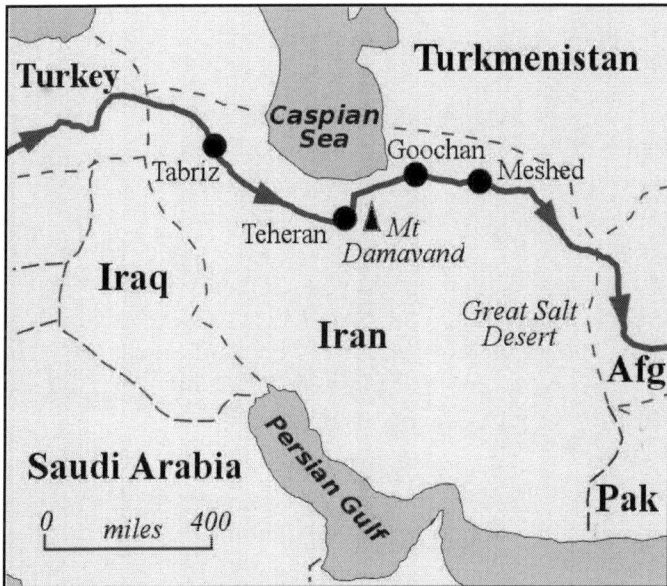

The "Carnet de Passage en Douane" was a customs document which allowed a vehicle to be temporarily imported into a country and guaranteed that it would be subsequently exported. Most countries on our route so far seemed to have ignored this requirement. However, Mike was not concerned, as we had obtained such a booklet of authorised carnets before leaving London. He carefully laid out the requested paperwork on the immigration counter.

"Thank you, sir," said the officer as he began to examine the passports.

Suddenly Mike froze.

His eye had wandered slowly over the pieces of paper, and on the front cover of the carnet he saw a list of countries representing our journey to Singapore. At the bottom of the list was an entry "Not valid for Iran"! All sorts of images flashed through his mind, as he realised the implications. Without a carnet we could not pass the customs desk. Either we would have to turn back, or pay a huge deposit for the vehicle, far beyond our ability. Would we have to return to Turkey? Was there any other way to the East? Might this be the end of the expedition?

Thinking more rationally, Mike realised that he had no control over the situation, and that his best course was to remain silent. So, based on this thought, he stood - outwardly patient but with beating heart - while the man scrutinised the licences and registration book. Finally, he picked up the carnet, and without a glance flicked it open. After writing for a while on various pages, he produced a large rubber stamp and gave three hard bangs into the booklet. Extracting one page for his records, he returned the carnet with a smile.

"Thank you, sir, you are finished."

Weak at the knees, Mike wobbled back to the car to report to me the close encounter of our journey with termination.

The Persians were charming and helpful at the border post, and we obtained some excellent maps and brochures from the Tourist Office there. Climbing back into the vehicle, we emerged onto a beautiful asphalt road - no rattles and no dust.

"Will it last?" I wondered. "Perhaps this is just to impress visitors, and we will be back to potholes and dust before long."

****

But my scepticism proved unfounded, as the splendid road continued, curving around the contours of the hills and plunging through tunnels between the valleys.

At one point we saw a group of women in brightly coloured dress and three imposing figures in white turbans. There were very few villages, mainly clusters of mud-brick houses.

Cooking lunch in pervasive dust at 35°C

It was very dry and hot. Fields of sunflowers drooped their heads towards the east, melons lay on the ground juicy and inviting, cattle and longhaired goats searched for food. We crossed a huge riverbed with an incongruous shallow stream of water trickling down the middle. The camels never failed to amuse us with their snooty airs, while the donkeys were certainly the beasts of burden. We saw one laden with two stripped tree trunks, which were dragging behind as he plodded along.

Since the van was not running smoothly, Mike adjusted the distributor points, which improved the performance. Coincidentally, a few miles down the road we came across two Pakistani men and a young lad peering under the raised bonnet of a small car.

"What is the trouble?"

"We're trying to get back to Karachi, but our car won't start."

After a brief inspection, Mike diagnosed the same trouble we had just experienced, reset the points for them, and soon they were mobile again.

On one stretch of road, we saw ahead of us a tall pile of grass on the verge, but as we looked it began to move. Getting closer, we made out two ears and a nose peeping out, and realised there was a donkey underneath - carrying a massive load.

****

On entering Tabriz, we found it to be a very smart modern city, which was obviously becoming tourist conscious. Beautiful flower beds welcomed us, and clear signposting took us to the smart Shah Goli camping area, which was in the process of being built into a terrific recreation centre with a lake, wide pavements for promenading, a picnic area and restaurants. The campsite ablution facilities were excellent.

We took a taxi into Tabriz city, and went to a restaurant which had been recommended to us. The excellent meal of tomato salad, thick chapatti, lamb cutlets, rice, chips and peas was most enjoyable, topped off by cream caramel and lemon tea. The taxi driver on the return trip was quite mad, and stopped to picked up some friends en route, who then sat in the back and laughed like jackasses.

Next morning Mike checked the van, and then we drove into Tabriz to look for someone to weld the bumper bracket. We found a very capable mechanic in the downtown area, and he appeared to do a good job of refixing the bumper. Later on, we were glad of that repair.

Driving into the city centre, we searched for a parking spot. There was the inevitable crowd of children round the van when we stopped. They were very attractive, with brown eyes and dark hair. Within the city, even the young girls wore long robes which covered them from head to foot. Usually this garment was brown with a floral pattern. The speech accent was soft, lacking the guttural sounds of Turkish. The bazaar seemed to have every item imaginable: spices, seeds, string, polythene rope, melons, kitchenware, clothes, subtly-shaded carpets, butter, biros, copperware, raw wool, shoes, bags and bales of cloth - to name a few! Bent old men pushed past, carrying huge loads on a kind of saddle on their backs. The domed ceiling of the market was roughly painted to give a brick effect. Each area was devoted to one commodity. We looked at the carpets, but we could not knock down the price. In the end, all we bought were six biro pens and a half kilogram of polythene bags. After a quick snack, we returned to the hunt for a tea-set for making "chay". Eventually we bought one fashioned in enamel, and made in Isfahan in southern Iran. In vain we tried to obtain a brass tea-maker, which is like a huge pot for boiling water, with a space for the teapot to keep hot on the top, and a tap on the side. Unfortunately, they were either too expensive or broken in some way. We contented ourselves with a tiny butterfly brooch and a pendant from the silversmiths.

Only gradually did a fact dawn on us, that should have been obvious - namely that the further east we travelled in the Muslim world the stricter did the cultural mores become. This was particularly significant in terms of my attire. In view of the hot weather, I had been wearing a knee-length dress as the coolest type of clothing, which by western standards was normal in summer. However, in central Asia it appeared that female knees were never on display, and this explained the constant sight of young men gawping at me. This was highlighted in two incidents. One was in a market where we were looking at various items, and I suddenly felt a sharp pain in my bottom. Glancing round, I saw a teenager who had obviously just pinched me.

"That guy has pinched me," I shouted.

"How dare he?" replied Mike, "I'll see to that!"

The offender dodged away through the stalls with the hunt in full cry behind him. The hunt was Mike. Soon they disappeared from my sight at the far end of the market. Ten minutes later my gallant knight reappeared, puffing heavily.

"What happened?" I asked anxiously.

"He took refuge behind his father's stall. When I indicated what had happened, the dad began to smack the boy."

"Poor fellow - all for one little pinch! Good thing you weren't arrested for chasing him!"

"You're right. I need to be more careful in future."

The second time that someone tried the same thing on me was when I was carrying a load of ice and fruit back to the van in a village. This time I was more prepared. As soon as I realised what was happening, I made a most unladylike movement. It would have suited David Beckham well, and the recalcitrant Iranian youth hurried off down the street, rubbing his sore bum.

As a result of these incidents, I decided that I needed to dress more circumspectly as we travelled through these cultures. So I climbed up to the chest on top of the van, and sorted through suitable clothing for the rest of the journey, donning trousers under my dress.

Selecting culturally-acceptable attire from the chest

We left Tabriz on an excellent tarred road, which passed through a valley, and then across a plain, before entering sandy-coloured mountains with deep gorges and dried-up river beds. Before long we were passing a series of spurs from the main massif, and the road dodged in and out of a set of tunnels interspersed with open stretches.

"The headlights don't seem very good," I commented while driving through one dark, unlit subterranean section. "Do you agree, Mike?"

"Maybe," was the reply. "Perhaps they are covered in dust. We can stop at the next bit of daylight."

So, between tunnels, we cleaned the headlamp glasses which were rather dirty, and then drove on.

"The lights still don't seem good," I complained in the next dark tunnel. "I can hardly see the road. Perhaps the battery is giving up!"

Shortly afterwards, I heard some strange sounds coming from my husband, and then recognised that he was engulfed in mirth. For a moment he could not control his hilarity, while I listened puzzled, and a trifle worried.

"Don't blame the headlamps," he gasped. "Take off your sunglasses!"

This incident kept us in laughter for many a mile after that, and shifted the blame from the poor battery which was continually being maligned.

We continued through many towns and saw a big effort to improve their appearance with well kept gardens, floral roundabouts and places to sit. In one town, which specialised in carpets, the items were hanging on the walls by the weavers' shops.

A village market in the Iranian countryside

****

As we approached Tehran we found ourselves on a modern motorway, but had to pay a toll for the use of it. Partway along this thoroughfare, the battery charging cut-out failed suddenly. As we proceeded, the lights gradually dimmed while we were searching along bad roads in the suburbs of Tehran for a campsite. Eventually we found the place just before the battery went completely flat.

Next morning it seemed that the cut-out system had rectified itself, and so having pushed the vehicle to start, we made a late departure, but were further detained by a serious lorry accident on a bridge. Because of the enormous traffic jam, vehicles gave up waiting and drove across the river bed instead. Eventually, we were on our way through the lorries and buses, and joined the chaotic traffic into Tehran city. It was like driving on a bumper-car floor in a fun-fair - and only just missing. We soon learned to drive in the same way in all these cities.

In this chaos we searched for the American Express office, to collect any mail that might have arrived for us. Finally we parked in the railway station, and picked up a volunteer who spoke the language and helped us to find the place. We flopped into a bar serving cold drinks and snacks, and settled down to read the letters from home - the test-match results, the wet summer and a minor political crisis. Lunch was a hunk of crusty bread stuffed with chicken, tomato and gherkin - washed down with fresh orange drink and ice cream.

We had much-needed haircuts, which were very expensive in the heart of the city. The Persian ladies in the salon were chewing gum while having full beauty treatments. The boss of the establishment had just returned from a European tour, and was full of praise for the ladies of London! The music of "Oh Happy Day", jazzed up almost beyond recognition, blared from the radiogram.

****

Late in the afternoon we drove north from Tehran to cross the pass through Mount Damavand, the highest peak between the Himalayas and the Rockies, and the second highest volcano in the northern hemisphere. Although there had been no eruptions in recent centuries, the presence of fumaroles suggested that the peak was still active.

The road was poor as we left Teheran, but improved as we drove higher, taking us through deep gorges leading to ranges of arid mountains. A few paltry cacti struggled for growth by the roadside. At last we could see the snowy crest of Damavand, and watched a tiny cloud drift across the volcanic cone. Lack of time and suitable clothing prevented us from climbing the peak or seeing the lake of ice in the crater.

The driving was still rather wild. A popular form of transport was the small Mercedes bus. This looked like a large dormobile with doubled tyres on the back wheels, and held about twenty people. One driver, whom we named Persian Percy, seemed particularly hyperactive. He overtook us, screeched to a halt while we overtook him, by which time his passengers had spilled out and he was roaring up behind us again ready for the next cycle of activity. In this way he passed us several times waving vigorously. After negotiating several tunnels we emerged into a river valley, which as darkness fell took us down to the coastal plain of the Caspian Sea.

We arrived in Sari, a very smart town with park areas illuminated with coloured lights. There were large numbers of students around, but a most unsavory group surrounded us when we asked a policeman where we could camp for the night. Not finding a suitable spot, we passed out of the town to an open-air restaurant on the outskirts. Having driven in through the gates, we sampled chicken kebab and rice, which was tasty enough but rather overpowered by the strong butter covering everything. While we were eating, a waiter brought us a note which stated in English that our high vehicle had broken two of the light bulbs as we drove into the car park, and asking us to take care when leaving. Our hopes of parking for the night there sank. On enquiring, we were given a firm reply in the negative. We drove out carefully, and eventually camped outside a house on the edge of a village at midnight.

We repeatedly attracted the interest of Persian youngsters

So far, we had found the roads in Iran to be of a very high standard, obviously the result of a major civil engineering push by the government. However, the map warned us that ahead lay a stretch that had not been rebuilt, between the Caspian and the Afghan border.

We left early the next morning, hoping to drive the major part of the unmade road in one day. The land was fertile with the Caspian lagoon in the distance on one side and the steep mountains on the other. On the map there appeared to be a shorter stretch of bad road to the north of the mountains than to the south, which was bordered by the Great Salt Desert.

We drove through the prosperous town of Gorgan where we bought some hot chapati unleavened bread, which we ate at a beautiful grassy location by the side of the road. Unfortunately, we discovered that the local goats also appreciated the quality of the grass - as well as our lunch. We moved on speedily. The mountains were thickly forested, interspersed with patches of dairy and arable farming. The corn was still green in this area, which seemed strange to us, as we had seen so much harvesting en route. Other crops included sunflowers and cotton, where the bolls were being handpicked. Many dragonflies flitted around like silent helicopters.

****

Just beyond the little town of Shahpasand we saw a cloud of dust ahead, and out of the cloud emerged a bus. We had reached the dreaded dust road of north Iran. The ground was gravel with desperate potholes and large boulders in the surface.

The "highway" through northern Iran

After about twenty miles with a maximum speed of 10 mph, the way improved, but continued to be very rough. The road passed through mountains following the course of a river valley, and we travelled through Mohammed Rez Shah wildlife park, where we made too much noise to see any wild creatures apart from a couple of birds, which flew away hastily at our approach.

Surprisingly, there was considerable traffic on this road, mostly heavy trucks, which threw up clouds of dust whenever they passed. I found it was better not to breathe in too hard to avoid choking, and we had to blow our noses constantly to remove the mud. It was encouraging to note for future travellers that a beautifully-surfaced road was being built near to the current route.

Realising that we would not complete this rough section of our route in one day, we stopped in the evening after covering 97 miles. A small plateau, which had been prepared when a cutting for the new road had been built, provided a suitable campsite in this lonely spot. Over our meal, Mike was perusing some leaflets we had picked up in a previous town.

"It says here that these mountains are hosts to some pretty rare animals - even cheetah, so it says."

In the middle of the night we were awakened by a snuffling outside, and the sound of our rubbish bin being overturned.

"Might be a cheetah!" Mike declared excitedly, fitting the flash unit onto the camera while reaching for the door.

"Don't be crazy!" I implored. "That could be a dangerous animal."

Reluctantly he accepted my logic, and we had to content ourselves with peering through the window into the darkness. But our movement seemed to have frightened our guest back into the hills. Next morning we found that something, or someone, had enjoyed a meal from our bin outside the van, leaving a trail of half-eaten remnants up the hillside.

We drove on through sandy mountains with patches of cultivation, although with no sign of water. Dust poured into our vehicle through every nook and cranny, and we were perpetually coughing and sneezing. Frequently the visibility through the windscreen became so bad that we had to stop and scrape off the layer of yellow particles.

At one point we paused so that I could photograph a camel, that we nicknamed Clarence. Every time I was about to press the shutter, he moved up the hillside a bit more. I chased him for quite a while, and eventually got a reasonable picture of this ship-of-the-desert, and not just his rear view.

My friend Clarence when he condescended to stop running

****

About 25 miles west of the town of Bojnoord, we were stopped by a small group beside the road, waving feverishly. Someone pointed to a fellow on the ground with a smashed jaw and injured hand, and managed to intimate that we should take him to the hospital in the next town. Carefully loading the patient onto the bunk in the van, we set off on our mission of mercy. After moaning for a while as we bucked along the unmade road, he fell asleep as we approached the town. Aware that there was probably no English-speaker in this remote place, we contented ourselves with drawing up beside the first group of young men in the main street, and gesticulating toward the interior of the van. Quickly they got the message, and one young guy jumped into the passenger seat, and pointed us through the maze of simple houses until we reached some sort of clinic. After an animated discussion, a uniformed nurse appeared with a trolley, and the unfortunate man was transferred to better care than ours. After leaving the town, we made good use of the next stream to wash the blood off our bedding.

The road wound through a broad valley at the end of which was a stretch of brand new tarred road. Some boys wanted money to let us go onto this pristine section. One lad brandished a stick, so I drove towards the old road and then swung around their little blockade and onto the new road. It appeared that the thoroughfare had not been officially opened to traffic, but a number of cars were venturing along it. A tar-laying machine pulled aside to allow us to pass. Further on, while I was still at the steering wheel, another group of boys repeated their trick to extract money from us. This time they had a line of old tyres across the road. Mike leapt out, much to their astonishment, and moved one tyre which rolled towards the river. I drove quickly through the gap while the rubber obstruction bounded down the hill and came to rest in the water. The lads danced with rage. With Mike climbing aboard, I pressed the accelerator down hard.

****

Soon after this, the newly-constructed section ended, and we were back on the old dust road again. A stone from a passing coach flew up and hit the windscreen. This was the third happening of this kind, but once again we and the window survived.

"What's that puffing noise?" said Mike abruptly. "Better stop and see."

Lifting the bonnet, we expected to see a mass of steam pouring out, but everything looked normal.

"Rev up the engine, please, Pam."

"Okay, I've got it. The air-filter has worked loose."

And so another enforced rest by the roadside took place, as Mike fitted a new clip to the filter, which was complaining about its rough treatment on these primitive roads. Half-an-hour later it seemed to be secured, and we vibrated our way onward. A phenomenon that we had not expected was that the dusty surface was severely corrugated by a series of transverse humps and dips, which made the whole vehicle go into a paroxysm of shuddering as we drove along. Conventional wisdom was that to travel fast over these corrugations was the best solution, but in our case the chassis made such awful sounds that we thought it would tear itself apart. So we plodded onward at about 10 mph.

On either side there were encampments of nomads with beautiful horses. Their women looked positively medieval with dresses and trousers under a robe wrapped around their shoulders and over their heads.

A man was praying by the roadside, a sight we had expected to witness often in the Muslim countries, but in fact saw only rarely. More obvious were the mosques, even in the smallest of villages.

****

After 262 miles of bad road at an average speed of 13 mph, we came onto a fine boulevard leading into the town of Ghoochan. Heading through the tree-lined streets, we found a petrol station, and then drove out of town towards Meshed.

Twenty miles from Ghoochan, I remembered that I had left my watch in the garage loo. We returned, and finding it on the windowsill, decided to have a meal of shish kebab in the local restaurant before travelling on in the dusk.

We stopped outside the town to adjust the lights and then found that the engine refused to restart. The battery was obviously flat. But, unlike our experience in Turkey where inquisitive lorry drivers came to give help, nobody stopped. So, philosophically, we deferred the problem until the morning, and prepared for bed.

Next day at dawn, three fellows cycled along the road and we indicated our situation, thereby persuading them to give us a push. Immediately the engine started and we glided along the beautifully-surfaced road. We were very appreciative after yesterday's slog through the dust, and sped through a broad fertile valley with a strange mixture of mechanised farming, donkeys for carrying goods, mud villages, sheep, goats, cattle and turbaned-men with small beards. We were intrigued by the way that some people managed to carry their belongings on their heads and in both hands at the same time.

We arrived in Meshed and found tree-lined avenues, a stream down the centre of the main road, and students lounging under the trees reading. The roundabouts had lawns, flower beds fountains and statues. A policeman stopped us, but indicated that there were no camping sites. He directed us towards a tourist office in the suburbs, where a very helpful girl in western dress, speaking excellent English, informed us that camping was allowed at Meshed Airport. We arrived very hot and sticky at the campsite within the airport grounds, and the local security man indicated that facilities were available all night. We watched the only plane of the day, a Boeing 727, landing.

Later we were invited into the control tower, which appeared very modern and well-equipped, despite the paucity of air traffic at the airfield.

In the evening we wandered over to a set of fountains playing on the roundabout nearby. There were four sets with many sequences and colours. Mike peered down the hatch at the controls of this impressive display, and suddenly an officious little man blew a whistle madly and came rushing over, expostulating profusely.

In the intense heat we cleaned the vehicle, and Mike greased the bearings and refitted the air-horn on the roof. One gardener, whom we ingenuously nicknamed Fred Nurk, watered the same patch of grass outside our vehicle for two hours, while staring intently at us. When Mike asked him firmly to move on, he assumed that Mike was being friendly and so went and fetched two of his mates to sit three metres away from the van.

While in the washroom of the airport, which was virtually deserted, a policeman decided to appear in the ladies' section during my ablutions. I gave a shout, and Mike hurried over, and then gave the officer a lecture. The response was a reply of "No more camping!", and so deciding we had better leave, we packed everything ready for departure. However, we could not comply with the policeman's request unless he helped to push the van to start it. At first he refused, but when we started getting out the stools to sit down again, he quickly changed his mind.

In Meshed we searched for a battery, but were surrounded by hordes of boys every time we stopped. At last we discovered a shop that would sell and fit the battery. Meanwhile I went to the post office, where the clerk tried to cheat me over some stamps. When I protested, he simply gave up and laughed, since it seemed that this was standard practice! We bought some electrical flex from a stall, but the shopkeeper did a conjuring trick and gave us three metres when we paid for seven.

****

Leaving Meshed, we stopped to view a beautiful blue-domed mosque, in an area where there were no houses but just a graveyard and a cafe. Unexpectedly, we found ourselves on a fine, new road heading towards the border, but the lack of traffic made us wonder if we were really on the right route. This splendid thoroughfare ended at a sign indicating we were three kilometres from the Afghan border. Immediately a soldier stepped out into the road and stopped us. He studied our passports for a while, looking unhappy.

"Where the Taiebad stamp?" he asked.

"What is that?" we responded.

"You go Taiebad first!" he said, indicating another road joining at an angle.

We then worked out that our newly-finished route had by-passed the town where the immigration office was situated, and so we had to return there to have our documents processed. On entering Taiebad we were stopped by another soldier, and then directed to a police office nearby for the required formalities. The door bore a sign indicating that the office would be closed until 7 am the next morning. We therefore parked by the roadside and slept in the vehicle right in the town. On the morrow we completed the formalities and headed towards the next border.

Chapter 7
Afghan Adventure

We were now entering the most mysterious region of Central Asia in the whole of our journey to the East. This was a land about which we knew very little, despite attempts at research before leaving London. We drove for twenty minutes across the no-man's land separating Iran from Afghanistan, a flat plain filled with mud-domed houses. A few people were begging by the roadside.

The men in the passport control and police office were disorganised and unfriendly. The whole place was crowded with people who had slept all night on the floor of the offices, as well as those who were continuously arriving by bus.

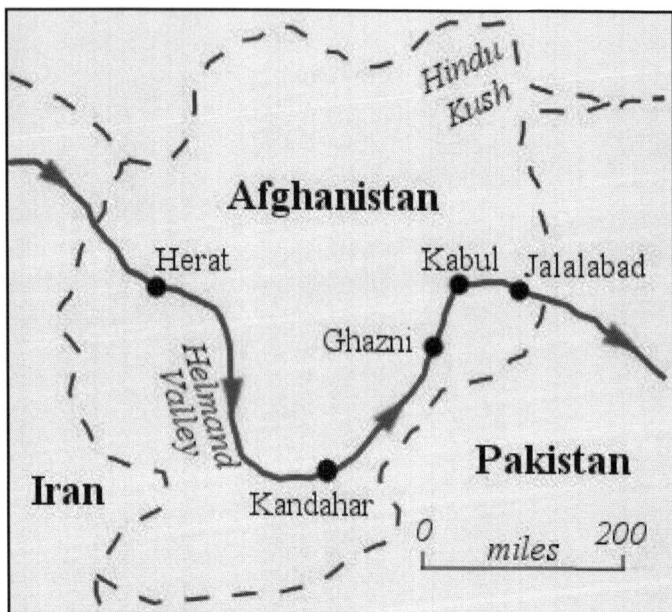

Hindu Kush

Afghanistan

Herat

Kabul   Jalalabad

Ghazni

Helmand Valley

Iran

Pakistan

Kandahar

0   miles   200

Some folk were very smart, particularly a man wearing a green dress and trousers, a brown waistcoat and a yellow skull-cap. The women wore white robes incorporating veils, and looking like spectres. The boys wore shirts and baggy trousers like pyjamas.

Although the passport and police offices were filthy and chaotic, it was a pleasant surprise to find that the vehicle insurance department was clean and tidy. Strains of Eastern music floated from the speakers, and the man himself was charming and helpful. Soon we were through with officialdom.

As we drove eastwards into Afghanistan, the first impression was sand. A strong wind blowing from the north caused drifts by the roadside, and the vista was yellow right to the horizon. We were amused by incongruous road signs indicating fords, but with a total lack of water there was no sign of riverbeds. As we travelled across the hazy plain, we could see Bedouin tents, horses, donkeys, sheep and camels - all indicating a nomadic people. A yellow scaly lizard scuttled across the road, and sandy-coloured birds with black undersides and long legs swooped overhead.

****

We reached the little town of Herat, which seemed to be an oasis in the desert. The wide avenues were tree-lined, and brightly decorated horses with painted buggy-carts trotted briskly through the streets. English was the alternative language over shop doors, although at times the spelling was rather amusing. "Greasing and Punchers" conjured up pictures of sweating, muscular men prancing around a boxing ring.

The town had a celebratory air, and someone told us that this was the festival of Jeshun. At the end of the main street was a large open-air stadium, and on approaching the entrance we were warmly welcomed to enter the packed amphitheatre. An attendant showed us to some prime seats, which suggested we were among the VIPs. Part of the display was incredibly dramatic horse riding by the army, followed by stirring marches and bands. The seating was interesting, since it appeared that all the upper class women and schoolgirls sat in the stands on the left, while all the male gentry were in the right-hand stands. The general populace was on the terraces. We were a little surprised and disconcerted when a young man explained to us in English the origin of this celebration. It was in remembrance of the expulsion of the British invading forces from Afghanistan in 1842. We quietly forgot to mention that we were British!

There was obviously nowhere to camp within Herat, and so in the late afternoon we drove out on the desert road. The landscape was flat apart from unusual mountains looking as though they had bubbled up from some underground reservoir.

Noting that there was no sign of habitation, we eventually stopped for the night at 11.30 pm beside the road. Although it seemed a lonely spot, we had a slight sense that perhaps we were being spied upon, and I had a distinctly creepy feeling about the place. So, as a precaution, we decided to sleep on the roof, and in fact were wakened in the middle of the night by footsteps walking around the vehicle. We held our breaths, and the night visitor disappeared.

As the sun came up next morning, we saw around us an awe-inspiring view of the endless desert, and were impressed by the range of colours that the early morning light produced. After breakfast, Mike refitted the bumper that had come loose again, and we proceeded along the excellent concrete road through the wilderness.

Twenty minutes later, a huge white animal came bounding out of the sand and ran along beside us for a while. It appeared to be a cross between a bear and a dog, and we kept the side doors of the van closed. After a while the animal swerved in front of us. Before we knew what was happening, we had hit it squarely.

A view of the desert where we spent our creepy night

After rolling over, it leapt up and ran away. Mike was inclined to stop after this accident.

"Don't be silly! I don't trust that creature - keep driving!" I exclaimed.

"All right. Anyway - good thing we fitted the bumper back this morning."

Later investigations suggested that the animal may have been an Anatolian sheep-herding dog, although whether it was wild or belonged to a village nearby we could not tell.

****

Both we and the vehicle were thirsty, and in the middle of the desert we found a sign indicating petrol. An indolent young man pumped petrol by hand from a machine, and then overcharged us by claiming that the meter was inaccurate. We then asked about cold drinks, and he showed us a refrigerator full of coke bottles. After purchasing a couple, we realised that this was not genuine Coca-Cola, but that the bottles had been refilled with some other brown liquid, tasting a bit like homemade beer. In disgust, we put the bottles down and climbed into the van. In a great rage the man ran towards us demanding payment as we made a quick getaway out onto the road. A short distance further on, we came to a toll booth, and wondered whether the jungle drums had been beating, and the angry young man had sent a message to stop us. However, the gatekeeper accepted our toll fee, and let us pass.

When we stopped for a break, we realised how completely silent the desert was - broken only by the flutter of a bird or the wind in the furtive scrub by the road. In the distance little dust devils rose and whirled across the landscape, and craggy, misty peaks of fairy-tale mountains appeared in the background.

Continuing along the fine concrete road, we repeatedly saw mirages of lakes on the hot surface ahead of us. Occasionally we glimpsed patches of purple, being bright desert flowers contrasting vividly with the brown and yellow around.

Our route through Afghanistan could not be directly from west to east, because of the impenetrable mountain mass in the centre of the country. Therefore we had to take the long desert road south from Herat to Kandahar and then make a U-shaped turn north again.

****

We arrived in Kandahar in the early evening. This town derived its name from Alexander the Great, who reached this area near the extremity of his eastward military expansion in the 4th Century BC.

It was a pleasant busy little place, although the signboard proclaimed it as "Kandahar City". We discovered that camping was allowed on the lawns in front of the Kandahar Hotel, and we settled down there in the welcome shade of leafy trees.

Wandering through the town, we rounded a corner and came face-to-face with a pair of European young men - both with dirty brown hair tied in pony-tails. Despite their appearance, they were friendly.

"Hey, you guys – where you from today?"

"Actually, we've come from Herat, through the Helmand Valley. Where are you heading?" I replied.

"We're en route to be happy in the Himalayas. Say, man! Come across any grass on the way?"

"Certainly not. It's absolutely dry right through. Just arid desert."

"See here, man. The grass is in the towns. You just have to look for it!"

In considerable bewilderment, we parted from the men, and entered a little shop. I bought a gaily-coloured shirt, after which the shopkeeper quite openly made an offer.

"You want hashish?"

"No thank you."

"Maybe opium - good opium from Thailand?"

"No - we prefer tea. Thanks, anyway."

"But all foreigners want hashish!" he expostulated.

And so we understood the strange conversation with the hippies, and that their grass was not the green kind. No doubt they would not turn down the shopkeeper's offer.

We retired for the night, sleeping on the roof under the mosquito net because of the great heat. At 1 am we were awakened by the sound of loud voices and vehicle engines. This continued for so long that we climbed down from the roof, and went to investigate.

"What is happening here?" Mike asked.

"Very bad, very bad," was the reply.

To our astonishment we saw a large Mercedes, which apparently had just been towed into the hotel forecourt by a tiny Austin Mini. The two drivers were conversing together looking severely shocked.

"I was driving through the desert after dark," explained the Mercedes owner, who was apparently a Pakistani. "Suddenly I heard a ping on the outside of the car - and knew someone was shooting at us. We huddled down, and heard bullets hitting the radiator – and next thing we knew was the car shuddering to a halt. We feared the worst - that the bandits would immediately attack us."

"You see," broke in the other driver, "I was following several miles behind. When I saw the stranded car, I stopped to give help. It seems my headlights frightened the bandits away. So I was able to tow his car into town."

Despite this sort of incident being relatively common in Afghanistan, it provoked discussion and analysis which lasted until dawn. When we remembered that we had spent the previous night alone in that same desert, we were thankful that we had emerged unscathed.

Next morning the town came alive very early, probably to beat the heat. Laden donkeys and camels headed for the centre, together with men carrying goods in baskets attached to yokes. The market stalls opened at 6.30 am. Buses rattled along with pieces of body work missing, exposing the engines. Many different types of costume were being worn, and we were particularly struck by people in Charles the First hats with cloaks pinned to one shoulder.

We left the town to drive north towards Kabul, from where we could make the crossing into Pakistan. It was much greener, and with more villages, than yesterday's drive, and for some miles the road ran beside a river. Great droves of camels and flocks of sheep grazed everywhere. There was much activity with hand-operated wells, oxen-drawn ploughs, and the clearing of irrigation channels.

Two modes of travel in rural Afghanistan

We commented repeatedly on the fantastic quality of the main road through Afghanistan. Only subsequently did we learn that the first stretch from Herat to Kandahar was the result of Russian aid, while the second part from Kandahar to Kabul was built with American funds. The Cold War had overtones even in this remote place!

On reaching Ghazni, we parked in a hotel forecourt with camping facilities, and then walked into town, which proved to be further than the half mile that we had been told. We tried the town bank for changing money, but began to realise that in Afghanistan the concept of Travellers' Cheques seemed virtually unknown. This forced us back to our meagre supply of U.S. dollars and Persian money.

Another problem we were facing was the heavy use of oil by the van. By this time we were emitting a plume of black smoke from the exhaust, and Mike learned from a garage that it was caused by the petrol. Apparently, all fuel came from Russia, and the smell of it suggested a close similarity with paraffin. By the time that we left Ghazni town centre it was really dark, and so instead of walking, we enjoyed jogging back to the van in a horse-drawn buggy.

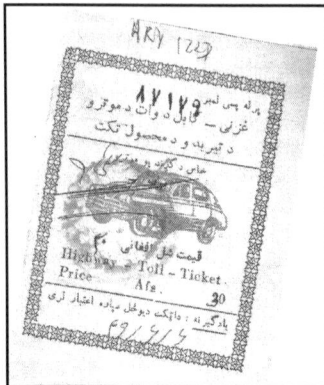

Currency and toll tickets were a challenge in these Arabic countries

Continuing north, we passed through a rugged mountain region with fertile pockets wherever streams were flowing. About every 30 miles we saw pairs of road-sweepers brushing the sand off the highway. Ruined castles and strongholds blended into the background of sandy-coloured slopes. A wandering drummer stood by the roadside at one point.

One perennial problem in this region was the propensity of little boys in the villages to throw stones at unusual vehicles. Several times we narrowly missed losing our windscreen or side windows. I developed a technique, probably from my school teaching days, of looking directly at a child who had picked up a stone, and pointing a finger at him. Usually, my blue eyes hypnotised him sufficiently for us to fly past out of danger.

Another issue which filled me with sadness was the plight of women in this particular society. Hardly ever seen on the streets, and then heavily veiled, they appeared to live a twilight existence on the periphery of society.

Two ladies of Kabul

I risked a quick photograph of two women sitting by a wall, but their dismissive head-shaking showed they were not happy - even for a female to take pictures of them.

The freedom of women to participate in national life had waxed and waned with the changing regimes in Afghanistan, but in 1970 their place seemed to be firmly fixed in the home.

A further reminder of life in this warrior nation occurred as we navigated through a remote village. A boy of about ten years of age was riding a donkey, while carrying a rifle that was taller than himself.

****

Crossing a pass, we saw below us the city of Kabul surrounded by mountains. Unable to find a suitable camping place in this fast bustling city, Mike phoned up a doctor whose name we had been given.

"Hello, could I speak to Dr Jock please?"

"I am sorry but he's out at the moment," was the reply of a young lady with a very British accent.

"Well, my name is Mike Collier - I was wondering if you could advise about somewhere to stay..."

A squeal broke into the conversation. "Not the one who was in Glasgow?"

"Well yes. How do you know me?

"I'm Pauline - we were classmates!"

"How fantastic!"

"Tell me where you are, and I'll come and meet you."

And so our weekend in Kabul changed immediately from our expectations. We were invited to stay with Dr Jock and his family, who made us very welcome, and gave us a dramatic change from the weeks of nomadic life.

This doctor was an incredible person, who had given up his medical career in Britain to run an eye hospital in

Kabul. Mike's friend Pauline was a nurse who was working as part of this far reaching project. Both of these were Christians who wanted to express their faith in practical care through the National Organisation for Ophthalmic Rehabilitation (NOOR), a body whose work was greatly appreciated by the Afghanistan government. It was a real inspiration for us to spend time with these folk.

Pauline gave us a tour of the Kabul bazaars, and having passed through several countries on our journey, we noted how each culture and ethnic group seemed to display its individualism in the style, content and atmosphere of its markets.

One of the many markets in Kabul

****

After such a stimulating break with such lovely people, we left Kabul to begin the descent from this city at 6000 feet through the Jalalabad valley. The road twisted down a narrow defile amid majestic mountain scenery with a tumbling mountain torrent beside us all the way. As we drove, we remembered the fact that this was the very gorge in which Lord Elfinstone's column of 16,000 soldiers had been annihilated by the Afghans in 1842 - leaving a sole survivor. One commentator called this event "the worst British military disaster until the fall of Singapore exactly a century later."

Passing through the small town of Jalalabad itself, we saw ahead of us the frontier post. We were reluctant to leave behind the beautiful Afghan roads, but not sorry to be free of Afghan petrol.

Chapter 8
Penetrating the Punjab

As we approached the Pakistan border post, we found ourselves at a rather interesting traffic junction. This was the point where left-hand driving took over from that on the right. Ever since landing in Belgium seven weeks before, we had kept scrupulously to the right-hand side of the highway. Now, on entering what had once been part of the British Empire, we found ourselves back on the familiar side of the road. The changeover was accomplished by a gate which allowed one car at a time to cross from one side of the road to the other.

As we queued up for the customs and immigration offices, we were beset by sly-looking fellows, who sidled up to us with the quiet whisper "Change money? Very good rate!" One young man came to chat to us in what was apparently English, but we had such difficulty in understanding him that he gave up with the retort "You don't speak English!" - and marched away in disgust.

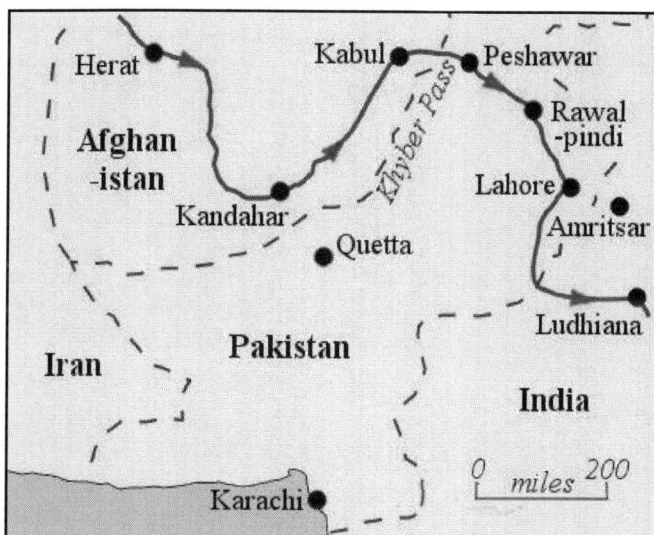

Soon we were chugging up the road towards the Khyber Pass, along a snakelike strip of tarmac which wound round the mountains to the main body of the pass. This ten-mile stretch bore many battle scars, and forts on the hillsides flanking our route reminded us of the turbulent history of this border. Many a conflict with mountain tribesmen had occurred here in colonial days. Even as we climbed, notices declared that the whole area was closed at night, apparently because it was still bandit-infested.

The zig-zag road leading to the top of the Khyber

The final ascent to the pass comprised a series of hairpin bends, and once over the top we looked down onto the green vista of the Punjab. Looking back at the brown and yellow shades of Afghanistan, we realised the enormous geographical difference between these two countries. Whereas the latter consisted of a high, arid tableland, the country we were now entering was really one huge well-watered valley.

As we descended the hairpins on the other side of the pass, I experienced a sensation that I had almost forgotten - the warm, sticky blanket feeling of a humid climate.

After the dry desert conditions of former weeks, this came as a shock.

****

On reaching the plain below we found ourselves among green fields and trees in a fertile farming area. Although the tar surface was not quite up to the standard of Afghan roads, it was quite adequate. We speedily arrived at the city of Peshawar - which in honour of its extreme humidity we nicknamed "Peshower".

The city strongly suggested the British influence which it had seen in the days of the Indian Raj. Large cool-looking residences adorned the hillsides, especially in the area of the cantonment, and the highways were meticulously laid out. After a search, we found that we could camp in the grounds of one of the main hotels. We settled down there, and I tried to cook a meal. But, with sweat pouring down my face and off my arms, it was an extremely frustrating exercise - and I became quite depressed. Mike noticed my battle with the elements, and slipped off to the hotel reception - returning with the news that he had managed to book a hotel room. We discovered that it was in fact a suite of three rooms, complete with electric fans and a very comfortable sitting room leading onto a large veranda. A heavenly change after recent weeks of roughing it!

After supper, which had been meticulously served by uniformed waiters, we wandered around the town. This comprised mainly small shops in a bazaar fashion. The local male dress was mainly long shirts and baggy trousers, with some men in western styles. The women were veiled, indicating how close to the Afghan border we still were.

****

After a good night in our comfortable suite, we set out again at about midday, southward through Pakistan. One impression we gained of the country was that it had plenty of water. In fact the name of the area derived from "punj" meaning "five" and "aab" signifying "waters". Thus Punjab referred to the five rivers, Jhelum, Chenab, Ravi, Sutlej and Beas, which were all tributaries of the Indus.

For many miles our road ran close beside the Indus, a wide swirling torrent. Peculiar rock formations sprouted from the river, apparently caused by the turbulent action of the water. Cotton-wool clouds rested on the beautiful mountains of Kashmir in the distance.

Verdant vegetation greeted us in the Punjab

On reaching majestic, colonial Rawalpindi, the home of the Pakistan army, we searched for a cheap hotel. The first one we tried was certainly cheap! But the toilets advertised themselves so pungently that we turned elsewhere. After a while, we found an air-conditioned room which was perfectly suitable.

Travelling across this country, I experienced an ambivalent feeling about the cultural ambience. On the one hand, it was definitely a Muslim country, evidenced by its mosques, veils and Arabic signs, while on the other it reeked of British influence in architecture, language and town planning. Whereas Iran and Afghanistan had a very consistent Islamic culture, this country seemed to be a hybrid of East and West – in some ways similar to western Turkey, perhaps.

For the first time on our journey, we came across English language newspapers - no doubt a tradition which had continued for over a century, despite the change from colony to independence. Even the style of the news reporting was similar to that of Britain thirty years before!

For the previous week, Mike had been getting worried about the amount of oil that the van was using. His analysis was that the crude petrol from Afghanistan had damaged the cylinders, with the result that we were burning and emitting both fuel and oil. The plume of black smoke that followed us seemed to confirm this theory.

"Well, as far as I can see, we have two options," he surmised, as we sat in our comfortable Rawalpindi room.

"Let's hear them, then!" I coaxed.

"One would be to have the engine rebored. That means taking the head off, and then milling the cylinders. We would need oversized piston rings, when we put it together."

"Sounds like the sort of job you could do by the roadside in ten minutes," I joked. "Anyway do they have facilities for this out here?"

"I'm pretty sure the local boys could do the job - it would be expensive and take a while."

"Even if you gave them a hand?"

"No chance. What with the language and their different methods – they wouldn't want me butting in."

"What's the second idea, then?"

"Looking back over the last few days we could work out current usage, and then extrapolate..."

"Extra what?"

"Make a guess how much oil we would use before reaching Singapore."

So with pencil, paper and map we "guesstimated" how much oil the van would consume for the rest of the journey. I worked out the total, which was not too encouraging.

"Twenty five gallons!"

"Oil or petrol? Well, what do we do?"

"Quite honestly, we haven't much choice," I mused. "We're tight on time – and we mustn't miss the boat from Madras."

And so we surveyed the garages in the city for the best deal, and then loaded twenty-five cans of lubricating oil onto the roof. It did not matter that the quality was poor, since it would soon be pouring out of the exhaust anyway! The vehicle sagged a bit, but we seemed to have found the best possible solution.

****

We set off again, following the Indus as it roared southward. Both of us were kept busy concentrating on the road, watching out for cyclists, pedestrians, crazy bus drivers and thundering lorries - plus camels, horses and oxen which formed part of the traffic. Even buffaloes and baby buffs grazed or wallowed right by the roadside. The driving standard was wild, and evidence of this was seen in three smashed cars and numerous dead dogs. Altogether an exhilarating ride!

Before leaving London, we had met a Pakistani student who was studying in the university there. When he heard of our proposed journey, he insisted that when we reached Lahore, we should call on his parents. He assured us that they would be very pleased to see us. At first we thought he was just being polite, but when he returned with a letter from his father inviting us to stop with them, we realised that it was a genuine invitation.

So, armed with an address, we drove into the city, finding it to be a vast maze. But our instructions were good, and eventually we arrived at a long, low bungalow right in the heart of the metropolis. The Patel family welcomed us warmly, and explained that they had prepared a room for us in a new house that they had built in the outskirts of Lahore.

Accompanied by one of the family members, we explored the area around their home. A book shop nearby proved extremely interesting with a large amount of material in English. As we left the Post Office, we were besieged by two insistent five-year-olds who tugged our arms while trying to persuade us to buy combs from them.

Since we were now in a country with a high interest in English, we had several lively conversations with young folk who could read the sign on the side of the van.

"Does that mean you are going to Singapore? That's a long way."

"That's certainly our plan."

"But you must go through India – a very dangerous place! People not nice!"

"We will have to go carefully then," we replied meekly, not wishing to get into a discussion of the sub-continent's politics.

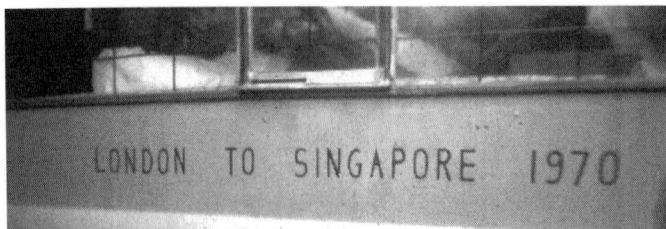

LONDON TO SINGAPORE 1970

In Anglophile Pakistan our sign generated some interest

In the evening, the Patel family treated us to a delicious Chinese meal in the Nanking restaurant. It seemed strange to be eating Chinese food in the midst of Pakistan, but it was extremely pleasant - both for the food and the company. After the meal they took us to the airport to view the facilities and the planes taking off and landing. It was certainly an active place even late at night. The only fly in the ointment was the unbelievably erratic performance of the family's driver, and we were glad to arrive back at our quarters intact. He was obviously trained in the School of Aggressive Driving, necessary for survival on Pakistan's roads.

The new house where we spent the night was a beautiful bungalow in a spacious area, and we awoke the next morning refreshed and ready to cross another border.

****

In view of the tense military standoff between Pakistan and India, the exact location of the border post kept changing. One could only find out where to cross a short time ahead of arrival. The Patel family discovered that

- 114 -

although the post was officially on the Amritsar road, it had been moved south to a place called Husainiwala about 100 miles distant. So we said adieu to our kind hosts, and headed out of Lahore.

The narrow strip of tar was crowded with lorries and buses, but surprisingly few cars. In a small village, we stopped before overtaking a parked lorry. As we did so, a frisky horse pulling a small cart, with hubs like Boadicea's chariot wheels, dashed through the gap, and crashed into the sliding door on the driver's side of our van. The owner of the cart whipped his horse into a fast trot and disappeared down the road. After considering for a moment what we should do, Mike reversed the van, turned around amid chattering villagers, and pursued the culprit until he brought the horse to a standstill.

With the help of a man in the crowd who spoke some English, we confronted the bearded driver, who admitted that the accident was his fault. Since this was the first country where we actually had no vehicle insurance, we felt it advisable to establish responsibility in this case, lest we be embroiled in legal problems later on. The man agreed to hand over five rupees, which was a pittance compared with the damage, but was a sufficient admission of liability. Because of the accident, the door would not close easily, but with a struggle we forced it shut until we could do repairs.

We then turned around, and headed on towards the frontier.

Chapter 9
The Grand Trunk

We negotiated the Pakistan border office easily, and set off across the "no-mans" strip between the two countries. After a couple of miles, we passed a sign indicating "Indian Frontier Post", and then slid into a large, muddy parking area. Mike asked a semi-official-looking person where the immigration and customs offices were, and was directed with a nod of a head towards a clump of trees. As was usual at border points, where petty criminals often lurked, I stayed to keep watch on the van, while Mike took the documents into the trees.

Twenty minutes later, he returned grinning broadly.

"Have you finished the formalities?"

"No - not by a long way. But you must come and see this! Otherwise you won't believe me."

So locking and alarming the van, I followed him into the copse. Once there, I looked around for the buildings – but there were none.

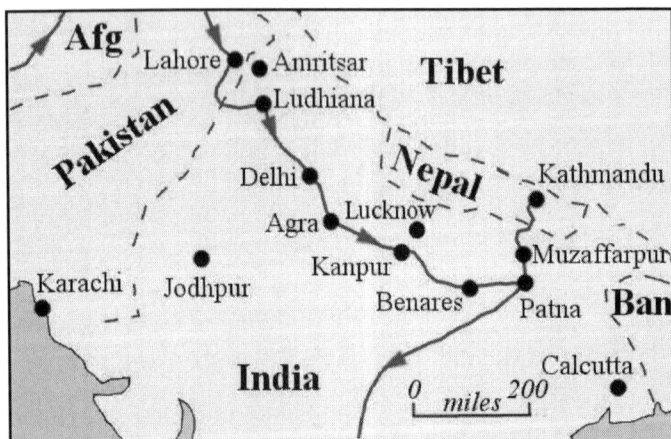

"Where are the offices?"

"See that little grey tent with the patches on it. That is the border post!"

In disbelief, I accompanied Mike through the trees and into the tent. The central feature was a large, uniformed gentleman sitting at a folding table. Standing around in silence was a circle of petitioners, and we noticed that as each one arrived he placed his passport on the table. For quite a while nothing happened, although the officer enjoyed his tea. Then, with studied insouciance, he picked up a passport, perused it at length, inked his stamp, banged it onto a page, and threw the document down.

Being prepared for a very long wait, we stood politely in the expectant circle. After a while the man noticed me, and then stared rather quizzically. One could almost see the man's thinking pattern on seeing a woman there.

"Well, I'd better impress these foreigners that India is better than the other side. We Hindus treat women better than those Muslims. I'll deal with her case first!"

So, impetuously, he grabbed our passports, and in lightning time processed them and handed them back to us. Thanking him courteously, we made our exit – leaving the waiting persons to wait.

****

Having crossed the frontier we drove onto a strip of road about one car's width. Very soon we realised it was advisable to move off the road whenever a lorry or bus approached, since these vehicles stopped for no man. Often the lorries were heavily overloaded, and therefore dared not move off the crown of the road. In some places there was a brick shoulder which provided a firm foundation, but in others the bricks had broken up. The roads were tree-lined with grass verges, but no houses with neat gardens lay behind - only fields of maize and rice with muddy tracks leading away to clusters of buildings in the distance. This was the Indian section of the verdant Punjab. Turbans of many colours dotted the road ahead, and Sikhs strolled along or travelled two on a bicycle. Old men with red turbans and white beards looked like Father Christmas in multiplicity.

On reaching Ludhiana, we searched for a Dak bungalow, since we had been told that this was one of the most convenient and cheapest types of accommodation for travellers in India. The word "dak" meant "mail" in Hindi, and these smart premises had been built in colonial days for mail couriers on their journeys across India. Although originally of a high standard, many had deteriorated, and so one could never be quite sure what one would encounter. In this case we found a very old one, which was sparsely furnished, but quite spacious and clean. Lizards darted across the wall, tiny frogs hopped about, and the electricity was intermittent. Outside in the evening light, chipmunks chased each other, while flashes of bright green indicated tropical birds.

Despite the intense heat, even in the evening, Mike took off the sliding door of the van to beat out the dents that we had received in the morning. Then, together, we tried to refit the door, which took us two hours of struggling before it would work again properly.

The road widened as we departed Ludhiana in the morning, and some hours later we stopped for lunch beside the road. We left the van doors open while we picnicked nearby. A group of friendly Sikh young people came to chat, and we discovered that they were reading quite advanced English books, but their comprehension and vocabulary were limited. While we were conversing, a boy from the group, but not a Sikh, quietly detached himself and slyly stole the compass off the windscreen and Mike's purse from a locker. Luckily the latter only contained a small number of rupees.

As we drove on, we spotted store houses made of mud beside the road, looking like inverted ice cream cones.

****

And so we entered New Delhi. Impressed by this very modern city, we soon discovered a confusing variety of modes of transport, both ancient and modern. The thoroughfares were crowded with cars, taxis, rickshaws, and tongas. Periodically the traffic came to a standstill because a cow, obviously of the sacred species, had decided to take a rest in the middle of the road junction. After searching unsuccessfully for campsites or places to stay, we resorted to the Ranjit Hotel, which was a fine, though not cheap, oasis from the chaos of the city. While walking around the streets, we were repeatedly accosted by a fellow who was very anxious to buy some of our belongings. Good quality clothes were difficult to buy in India, he told us.

The challenges of city driving in India

Next morning, we left the hotel and threaded our vehicle through the maze of streets, until we reached the road towards Agra. Having left early, we were hungry, and stopped at a sign offering breakfast at the Canal View Cafe. The restaurant looked modern by Indian standards on the outside. Once inside, our eyes took time to get used to the murky gloom, and we noticed that the tablecloths were attached to the tables by cobwebs. We ordered fish, which we hoped was not locally caught, and then sat back and waited.

Suddenly something fixed itself to my toe. I shook my foot and screamed. It disappeared. The manager saw my leap into the air, and came over to enquire about the problem. I asked him whether there was a dog or cat in the room, because I had felt something.

"No problem - it's only a rat," he replied nonchalantly.

We swallowed some of the fish, drank two mouthfuls of thick black tea from the grimy-looking cups, sipped gingerly from some lemon squash, paid 12 rupees, and fled. The manager followed us out quickly with my sunglasses, which I had left behind in my haste.

****

After several hours we entered the city of Agra, well known to students of the history of the colonial Raj. It was here that we hoped to make an encounter that we had planned well in advance, but in the bedlam of the town's streets we wondered if we would be successful.

As we drove cautiously through the town, we suddenly saw an arm waving vigorously out of the maelstrom of humanity. A slim European lady jumped into the road ahead of us, gesticulating madly. Mike slammed on the brakes, as she wrenched open the passenger door and leapt on to the bench seat next to me.

"Where have you been all this time?" was her first question.

"Pam, let me introduce my Aunt Margaret!" said Mike with mock formality.

The lady hugged me vigorously.

"It's wonderful to meet you at last, Pam!" she enthused. "I've heard so much about you - and it's great to see you face to face."

"Where shall we go now?" asked Mike.

"I came here about a week ago, expecting you, and so booked into some rooms at the Methodist church compound. Follow this road, and I will direct you."

Soon we were ensconced in a very pleasant, simple room, which had been prepared for us. It was clean and bright, with a view out onto the courtyard of a secondary school, where uniformed Indian students were at work and play.

Over a very welcome afternoon tea, we chatted animatedly about a whole range of subjects. Mike's aunt was actually a doctor, who early in her career had gone to the Belgian Congo. For decades she had run a hospital in the deep forest of the upper reaches of the Congo River. There she had become increasingly active in treating leprosy patients.

When independence came to that country, the ensuing violence had caused foreigners to flee in a hurry, leaving everything behind. Dr Margaret had then turned her face to India, which was a country with a huge leprosy problem. Being an acknowledged specialist in that field, she had established a leprosy treatment hospital in the north-eastern state of Bihar. It was our plan now for her to travel with us back to her centre.

At the conclusion of the leisurely tea and chat, Dr Margaret went onto the street and hailed a pony and trap. Then we had a memorable jog through the streets of Agra, until we came to the famous Taj Mahal.

I was overwhelmed by the sight of it, which defied description. It was probably the finest building I had ever seen - an exquisite marble structure silhouetted against the pale pink evening sky. The Mogul emperor Shah Jahan had built it as a memorial to his wife Mumtaz, who died giving birth to her fourteenth child.

The Taj Mahal in all its splendour

After dusk, we rode back through the bazaar to a supper of buffalo meat, followed by guavas. Returning to our room, we struggled through a pile of washing using cold water in a kind of trough in the bathroom - and collapsed into bed exhausted.

After an early morning service in the church next day, we drove back to see the Taj Mahal again. The received wisdom was that it should be viewed at three times of the day in differing lights to fully appreciate the detail and colouring – at dusk when it is pink, noon-time when it is white, and moonlight when it is ethereal. On this occasion, we passed through the sandstone entrance arch into the main compound, fought our way through the guides and post-card sellers, and strolled beside the endless line of lily ponds until we reached the front of the mausoleum.

Being daytime, it was now open to the public, and we joined the queue to see the interior. But we found it disappointing. The actual tombs of Shah Jahan and Mumtaz were below ground level, and only stone replicas were visible in the large empty vault. Compared with the intricacy and beauty of the outside, the actual tomb-chamber was rather plain.

The inside was not as awesome as the exterior

Being a fluent Hindi speaker, Dr Margaret was able to introduce us to a number of esoteric experiences. One surprise, as we left the Taj, was to go to a restaurant where she ordered a "Killer Diller" ice-cream. This turned out to be a highly exotic version of a knickerbocker glory, and was obviously a local favourite!

We then drove 26 miles out of Agra through small villages, to the beautiful, deserted city of Fatehpur Sikri. This was built on a lonely hill which rose above the plain. The story is that a Sufi mystic lived with the stonecutters in this small town. The emperor of the time desired a son, and asked for the holy man's blessings. Soon after the birth of his son, Emperor Akbar decided in appreciation to move his capital to Fatehpur. The city took five years to build, but after sixteen years was abandoned. The shortage of water no doubt contributed to its downfall, for Akbar had such a vast court. As we gazed at these huge deserted buildings, the evening light softened their sandstone appearance. We visited the remains of the summer and winter palace, the mosque and tombs. The emperor was a great innovator, and established a girls' school, in front of which we saw the Pachisi Board, made up of paving stones with the emperor's stone seat in the centre. This was used for playing a game, not unlike chess, where the emperor used slave girls as human pieces to be moved around the board. We also inspected the building where Emperor Akbar played hide-and-seek with the ladies of the court.

Looking down the hill, we saw a lad running towards us, and he brought news that the burglar alarm on the van was going off. Immediately Mike outran Roger Bannister, as he belted back down the slope to the vehicle. Drawn by the screeching of the air-horns, a crowd had gathered, and men were peering into the engine, but it appeared that nothing had been broken or stolen.

One man was explaining to Mike in broken English that there was something wrong with the van, when Dr Margaret arrived at the scene and reprimanded the crowd sternly in Hindi about the fact that somebody had tried to break into the vehicle. This curtailed our visit, although we had seen most of the sights of Fatehpur Sikri, and we drove back into Agra through heavy rain. At one point we caught sight of a jackal, which slunk away into the darkness.

****

According to the map, we were driving along the Grand Trunk Road of north India. This description puzzled us, for the surface was bumpy and narrow in many places.

But suddenly, in the distance, we saw the answer. For coming along the Grand Trunk Road was the Grand Trunk itself! It was, of course, an impressive pachyderm, complete with mahout. The man was kind enough to stop and introduce his four-footed friend. He explained that the load on the animal's back was one day's supply of food for him. Chuckling heartily over this new meaning of the route's name, we continued on our way.

The Grand Trunk on the Grand Trunk

The three of us continued to drive east along this prestigious highway, amid the usual traffic of pedestrians, bicycles, buffalo, sacred cows, sheep, and speckled goats with kids.

An ingenious and tiring method of lifting water

A man was using a primitive, but very effective, swinging water pump to irrigate his fields, employing a technique that must have been in use for centuries. In the fields crops of maize, sugar cane and rice were nearing harvest.

I noticed much more animal and bird life in India compared with earlier stages of our route. Egrets and vultures were cleaning a carcass, while storks stalked about in the fields. What appeared to be herons with vermilion-coloured heads flapped across the landscape, and a group of mongooses and chipmunks squabbled nearby.

One evening we came into a town after a long stretch of dust road, and were informed that the dak bungalow was near the railway station. After driving through muddy puddles, and reversing this way and that, we found that the accommodation was occupied. Then we were directed to the military bungalow, and the caretaker there, called a chowkidar, agreed we could spend the night at the place.

A terrific squawking from the back room indicated rats, cats, chickens or something worse, and the building was in a bad state of repair. After taking one look, we decided to sleep on the roof of the van instead. Dr Margaret stoically moved a bed under a fan in the hall of the bungalow, and slept there.

By the time that we had settled into our new accommodation it was after 10 pm, and so we dug into our supplies and made a quick meal of spaghetti bolognese, pineapple, cheese and biscuits.

The ablutions were in an outbuilding inhabited by a goat, and were of the typically Indian type. Happily, the chowkidar produced a bucket toilet which was a moderate improvement.

From there, our route took us into the holy city of Benares, where we gazed at Mother Ganges, the river which is supposed to purify all that is thrown into it. We stood on the ghats, where bodies were cremated and absorbed by the river, while at the same time we watched a man washing his hair in the water.

Nearby, a boat was anchored, with men and women walking along a plank to the shore with building materials balanced on their heads. Unfortunately there was only one plank, so those carrying sand were impeded by those returning with empty baskets. We left the riverfront, resisting the persistent pleas of a boatman to take us on a sightseeing trip by water.

A rainy day in Benares

Leaving the city, we headed onward in search of accommodation for the night, which was made more difficult by a very heavy storm. At last we found a tourist bungalow several miles outside the town. It was situated in a beautiful garden, and pleasantly decorated, but the power supply had been cut off - so we had to manage with our little Gaz lights and stove.

Lizards darted across the wall and ceiling, and I am sure that one missed his footing, and fell on me during the night. I awoke covered in bites from "little things" in the bed.

The following night we stayed at the Holy Family Hospital run by Catholic sisters, and had an excellent meal and a comfortable room. It was my first ever stay in hospital, and it was very enjoyable!

We were entertained in the recreation room, which was comfortably furnished and had a stereo record player. Next morning, following breakfast, the sisters gave us a huge polythene bag of food with the comment "In case you are stuck by the roadside".

Soon after leaving, we saw the results of a bad accident in which a cabinet minister, his driver and two passengers were killed. Apparently a bus pulled out to avoid a child and hit the car. Immediately, the driver pulled off his uniform, and ran away. We heard that he later gave himself up at the police station.

In the light of this, Dr Margaret advised us that if possible one should never stop after an accident in India, because injuring a sacred cow or a local person might result in being lynched by the villagers. The safest procedure was to continue to the next town and report to the police station. We saw four other wrecked cars on the road in this section of our journey.

****

Having an expert on Hindu language and culture with us made our journey so much more interesting. For example, we were intrigued to see whole lines of people walking out of the villages along the roads each evening, each carrying a small brown water-pot. We asked what it was all about.

"The reason is that it's against Hindu religion for people to excrete in the same place. So all the people go to the outskirts of their village daily," Dr Margaret explained.

"What about the little pot?"

"It's called a lotah – and each person has their own."

We also noticed twigs being cut off certain types of tree, and enquired about this.

"These are used as toothbrushes. In the towns you can see hawkers laying out their twig toothbrushes on the pavement for sale."

"How about the legal and governmental system?"

"Sadly, as far as I can see, the courts in India are generally corrupt - with cases often taking five years to complete. There is so much bribery that no witnesses can be considered truthful. In fact, most cases are settled out of court. In general, Indian administration could be described as 'bureaucracy gone mad'."

When we talked about the traffic which we saw, she explained that no imported cars were allowed in India at that time. A model based on the old Morris Cowley was manufactured in the country, and sold for about £1400. Arrangements with the Fiat company resulted in locally-made Fiats being available. There was also a car called the Standard, which was based on the Triumph Herald, produced in India. On the roads there were many trucks and buses, but comparatively few cars.

We saw very few children's toys. A little girl was playing five-stones on a shop floor, and we spotted several kites. In one village, we observed a big wheel with little chairs on it, made entirely in wood - probably by the local carpenter.

****

After a long haul across north India, it was with great relief that we arrived at Muzaffarpur, where Dr Margaret's hospital was situated. We were warmly welcomed into the bungalow which she shared with the two European nurses who were part of her team. It was a cool, light and spacious building, and our bedroom had the most enormous en-suite bathroom imaginable. Dinner that night was roast goat, which tasted just like lamb, and accompanying vegetables. Really delicious!

Dr Margaret's colleagues came from Australia and the UK, both being specialists in leprosy treatment. The town itself was a large flat metropolis, dominated by a massive railway junction. The hospital was some way from the centre, and occupied a pleasant site with plenty of open space.

Dr Margaret at her leprosy hospital in Muzaffarpur

On our second day there, we were invited to the hospital itself, where the patients had prepared a reception for us, as honoured visitors from the doctor's family. At the gates we were greeted by a huge crowd of staff and patients, all pressing their palms together in traditional Indian greeting, and saying "Namaste". A group of smiling women came forward with huge garlands of flowers which soon found their way round our necks. Despite the horde of people, we felt the atmosphere was like that of a big family, which made us feel very welcome.

The whole medical operation was most impressive, with large numbers of airy wards for the patients, and well-equipped operating theatres and treatment rooms. Dr

Margaret was a person with a great caring heart for those in need. In contrast to some others in her field, she believed that leprosy itself was not highly contagious, as long as strict hygiene was maintained. For that reason, she was quite willing to touch her patients while diagnosing and treating them.

We saw workshops where special shoes and other aids were being made to help the leprosy sufferers live more normal lives. Our hearts were really touched to see this dedicated group of Europeans and Indians working together to meet an on-going need of the Indian population.

After our tour of the hospital, we returned to the bungalow with lots of questions about leprosy and its treatment. Despite the isolation of the place, Dr Margaret was keeping up with western research in new methods of treatment, such as the use of sulphur drugs. We understood that she was well-known and respected at an international level. Personally, we were grateful for all the time that she devoted to us out of her busy life.

Chapter 10
Nepal Excursion

Although our way to Singapore would lead us down through the south of India, we were so entranced by the hidden kingdom of Nepal, that we decided to make a brief trip into that hidden land.

Armed with maps and advice from Dr Margaret, we set off from Muzaffarpur northwards towards the Himalayas. We passed some fishermen punting along a river, and then spied a mongoose scuttling across the road. Bihar was one of the poorest states in India, and many of the children ran around naked. The men were draped in off-white robes, while the women wore saris. As darkness fell, our headlights picked up hundreds of frogs hopping across the road.

After a comfortable night in Raxaul with some friends of Dr Margaret, we departed in pouring rain across the border into Nepal.

At first the road was narrow but fairly flat, and large numbers of lorries made our progress very slow. After 23 miles we passed the smart little town of Hetaura, and the road started climbing slowly up through beautiful forests.

Majestic mountains surrounded us, and red and yellow butterflies flitted above the flowers. We caught sight of a few birds, but were unable to identify them - possibly a yellow-breasted wagtail and a grey-spotted bird a little larger than a blackbird.

The Nepali people in the villages were light-skinned with broad faces, contrasting considerably with most of the peoples of the Indian plains.

Nepal lay right in the heart of the Himalayas, and was crossed by two great east-west ranges of mountains. On the northern border lay the Great Himalaya Range, incorporating the major peaks such as Everest. In parallel with this to the south stood the Lesser Himalaya Range, which our little vehicle was now trying to scale.

Up and up we crawled - at times with the engine racing in first-gear. After five hours of slow crawling, the vehicle became very sluggish. We were at a height of 7000 feet, and had to stop to let other vehicles pass us on one of the steeper sections. When we tried to pull away, the engine died. A few young road workmen tried to give us a push, but still the gradient was too steep. Mike checked the points, cleaned the plugs and dismantled the carburetor, but still the van could not move uphill. A passing motorcyclist stopped to inform us that the thin air at this altitude often affected the pulling power of a vehicle. His analysis seemed plausible, especially after the effects of Afghan petrol on our engine over recent weeks. We were almost at the highest point of the journey, but nothing would persuade the van to climb the last few hundred feet. Driving in reverse was also attempted, but the gear ratio was no lower than first-gear. We envied the five-gear trucks roaring past us up the pass, while our three gears were insufficient.

At 4 pm we decided to return to Hetaura, where we had noticed a U.S. aid base. Carefully doing a multipoint turn on the narrow road, we began to descend back the way we had come. Away to the west we saw a beautiful sunset over the rugged mountains. The radiator was now leaking badly, and so we were forced to stop at streams to fill up the water containers.

On arriving back in Hetaura, we drove straight to the U.S. base, which was being manned by Nepali staff. Explaining our predicament, we asked if we could leave our vehicle in their care while we tried to take a bus over the passes into central Nepal. They checked our nationality from our passports, and then agreed that we could park on the lawn in front of one of the offices.

The next morning I cooked some rice, and packed a tin of corned-beef from our emergency supplies. Then, with rucksacks on our backs, we inquired about bus services to Kathmandu. There was one leaving at 9 am - and after a while an ancient Mercedes charabanc rattled to a halt. We paid the fare, climbed aboard, and took our seats for a journey over the top of the world. It was slightly disconcerting to find that the bus had no self starter, and that a group of the passengers had to push the vehicle in order to get underway.

Later we realised there was also no hand-brake on this vehicle! In contrast, the engine was spotlessly clean and the vehicle had five gears. Whenever we stopped for a break, the driver would either leave the engine running, or park at the top of a hill and put the bus into gear.

Slowly we retraced the miles of the previous day, until we recognised the place where our van had rebelled. This time we continued to climb slowly up to the summit of the pass, and then began the descent to the valley below. We appreciated our cold lunch of rice and corned-beef.

Wooded mountainsides rose up to left and right of us. On the lower slopes, terraced rice and maize fields could be seen. There were many wildflowers growing on the banks by the roadside, and we manage to spot one orchid.

In the distance we could see a group of black mushrooms by the side of the road. But as we came nearer we realised that they were Nepalis crouched under black "city gent" umbrellas in the pouring rain.

There were more villages in this area, with the houses built of mud bricks and having thatched roofs. Maize on the cob and red peppers were hanging from the balconies to dry.

Ticket for a mountain bus with no handbrake or self-starter

At one point, where the mountain road traversed a steep hillside, we found that a whole section had fallen away into the valley below. A small army of peasants was chopping away at the rock face to make a ledge along which traffic could pass. Our bus wheezed its way over this slippery mud track with the right-hand windows hard against the cliff and the left overhanging the precipice below.

One Nepali gentleman on the bus provided us with some bizarre information about the road we were using.

"You know - in building this road across the ranges, the route had to be chosen to avoid a number of holy places. The local people had raised strong objections."

"So this accounts for the tortuous course that it takes," concluded Mike.

"Exactly. But there are still some disturbing rumours about."

"What sort of rumours?"

"Well, I don't know for sure. Nobody is sure. There are stories that human sacrifices were made at specific points. It seems the spirits needed appeasement."

"Ugh! What a grisly idea!" I commented.

The bus took us over a second pass into the Kathmandu valley, but it was sometime before we saw the city itself. After eight hours of grinding gears and steaming brakes, we finally jumped off the bus into a rickshaw to look for accommodation.

A guest house had been recommended, which we found without too much difficulty. It was an orphanage run by a single lady, who offered us a very suitable room for two nights. Wearily, we dropped into bed, leaving the sight-seeing for the morrow.

****

Refreshed and ready, we set off the next morning to explore Kathmandu. Despite its remoteness, it had a surprising mixture of cultures. A football game was in progress in a stadium, and a motley collection of vehicles crowded the roads.

In terms of belief, there was considerable variety. A Buddhist stupor, with its domed roof and four pairs of eyes looking out over the city, stood near to a Hindu shrine. Throughout the city there was also evidence of Christian organisations performing medical and educational work.

Shades of syncretism: A Buddhist Stupor...

... and a nearby Hindu shrine

We found a Chinese taxi driver who spoke a little English, and was willing to drive us to some of the main sights in the valley.

First we went to the Nyatapola Temple, one of the highest in the world, built in 1708 AD. The Hindu taxonomy of existence was depicted in a series of statues leading up to the main entrance.

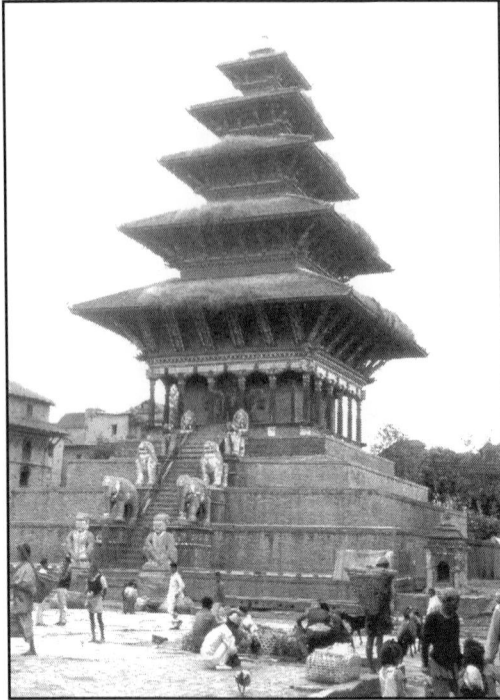

The Nyatapola Temple

At ground level there were two semi-human images, believed to be ten times stronger than the ordinary men in the courtyard. On the second step were two elephants, ten times stronger than the beings below. The next step had two lions, then two griffins, and on the top level sat two of the goddesses of the Hindu world. Each stage represented a ten-times increase in power, authority and spiritual strength.

It was quite thought-provoking to be at the bottom of this staircase among the humble humans.

Each level ten times stronger than below

We visited the Pashupatinath Temple, although only Hindu Pilgrims were allowed to enter the inner courtyard. The River Bagmati flowed through this temple, and then down to join the sacred Ganges in India.

Alongside the river were stone platforms similar to the ghats of Benares. Each morning, bodies of those who had died were laid on these and cremated, with the ashes being poured into the sacred river.

The Pashupatinath Temple in Kathmandu

The ghats where cremation took place each morning

Our taxi took us along part of the new Chinese road which ran from the Tibetan border to Kathmandu, past modern factories mainly making bricks and shoes. A large poster displayed a message from the King of Nepal, "More work can be obtained by persuading and convincing than by coercion and threatening." An interesting concept - worth thinking about! We completed our tour of Kathmandu during the afternoon in torrential rain, having explored the bazaar and main streets of the city.

On seeing a very ancient Austin Seven, similar to one that Mike had owned, we enquired about its origin. The owner was very happy to chat about his vintage wonder.

"How did this car get here?" we asked. "Did it come over that mountain road?"

"Yes and no," was the answer.

"What do you mean?"

"It came into Nepal long before that road was built."

"How come? – if there was no road."

"The original owner had it shipped from Britain to India. There it was dismantled, and each piece was carried by porters over the passes to Kathmandu. Then it was reassembled – and it's run for years in this valley."

"What about fuel?"

"Same thing. Carried over the hills. Today, of course, we have tankers that come in."

****

We were told that it would be cheaper and faster to return to India by obtaining a ride on a truck, rather than using the bus. Our pet Chinese taxi driver took us down to the lorry park, where he bargained for us, resulting in places costing 15 rupees each. We climbed into the front seats, while the other passengers travelled on the roof. The driver was Burmese, and spoke a smattering of English.

Shortly after starting, the vehicle stopped for a break at the Everest Point Restaurant. From there we could make out the snows at the very top of the world, and I was sure I could distinguish the peak of Everest on the skyline.

Arriving back in Hetaura, we rushed to the U.S. aid centre, where the staff seemed pleased to see us. I think they wondered whether we had dumped our van and would not return. We drove carefully back toward Raxaul, filling up the radiator about every five miles, and stopping to replenish the water supply at every river.

We returned across the border to Muzaffarpur, where we were welcomed back into Dr Margaret's homely bungalow. That night we were invited for dinner with some of her Indian friends, Dr Tenaja and his family, who gave us an excellent meal with dishes that were completely new to us. Indian food was very spicy, but Mrs Tenaja had remembered that we were not used to this, and provided only moderately hot dishes.

The next few days were spent in preparing the van for the long journey down the length of India. Mike took the radiator into the town, where it was resoldered - in what had become virtually a fortnightly ritual. He changed the two front springs, which were gradually surrendering in the fight against bumpy roads, and we gave the interior of the van a good clean. We did not expect it to remain in that pristine condition for very long.

Chapter 11
Indian Backbone

Rather reluctantly, we left the privacy and comfort of Dr Margaret's home for the long drive to the south of India. The staff of the bungalow turned out to say goodbye, and once again we found ourselves wearing garlands of colourful flowers.

For some time we had discussed the best route to the south. One possibility was to follow the east coast of India, but it would probably be very hot and sticky, and it was likely that many rivers would be in flood, impeding our progress. The alternative was to drive down the central mountain range, which would be much cooler and more scenic, although the road conditions might not be so good. Finally, it was decided we would take the second route, and so we departed from Muzaffarpur, full of curiosity about what the central spine of India would be like.

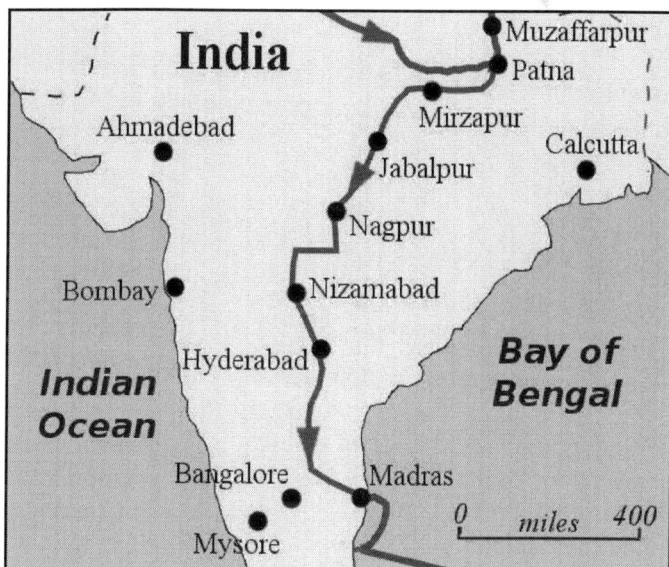

India
Muzaffarpur
Patna
Ahmadebad
Mirzapur
Calcutta
Jabalpur
Nagpur
Bombay
Nizamabad
Indian Ocean
Hyderabad
Bay of Bengal
Bangalore
Madras
Mysore
0   miles   400

On the first day we reached Chunar, travelling back up the Ganges valley. Arriving in the town, we began the hunt for accommodation for the night.

The only Hindi sentence that I had learned was "Dak bungala kahaan hai?", meaning "Where is the dak bungalow?". We stopped to ask a passer-by.

"Yes, turn right and drive one mile," he responded in excellent English.

Pausing a little later to confirm, we inquired again, with the reply, "Go straight on, turn right, right and right again. Take a left hand fork."

After all this, we arrived at a fort at the top of a steep hill. When we asked if we could spend the night there, the soldier on duty woke the officer-in-charge.

"You must acquire a permit from the town."

Down to the town we went, and made numerous inquiries to find the relevant office. Eventually a young lad jumped into the van to show us the place. After we had inquired about a permit, the clerk said, "I cannot give you permission. You must get it from Mirzapur."

Muttering under our breaths "Bureaucracy gone mad", we drove three miles back to the main road, and another twenty miles to Mirzapur. We failed to find the relevant branch of officialdom, but did find a dak bungalow with a vacant room.

The odour in the room was not to be described, and the murky water in the bucket was hardly suitable for washing - so we used our own supply from the van. The bowl in the washstand had a leak, so one's feet were washed simultaneously with one's face.

The chowkidar heated our tins of meat and beans. When this was mixed with some instant potato, we ended up with a very English meal, followed by pomelo. This citrus fruit with a thick skin, tasting like a cross between a grapefruit and orange, was becoming increasingly plentiful, and we became quite addicted to it. For the night, we moved our bed under the swaying fan, banged the bed hard so that the majority of the bugs would fall out, and arranged our sleeping bag. After removing a beetle from the latter, we dropped in and fell asleep at about midnight

Next morning we climbed sleepily out of bed, and were greeted by a fat frog which jumped out of a hole in the bathroom wall. Two of his offspring evaded our persuasion to drive them out of the door. I had the quickest wash of the whole journey, and we packed up very fast. Outside, a chap was preparing himself, Indian style, for the day ahead a few metres from the van. Two dogs insisted on sniffing around us all the time. I gave the chowkidar a four-rupee tip, but ignored his plea for more. The dark brown water of the Ganges flowed past the bottom of the garden. By 6 am we were driving out of the gates of the dak bungalow.

****

At this point, we turned away from the humidity of the Ganges valley and began to climb up into the central mountains. It was a beautiful area, and much less populated than our previously-experienced parts of India. We ascended to the plateau through forested hills, and noticed the dark-skinned, thick-lipped tribal people of the area. The tribal women wore their saris over blouses, and usually the garments were dyed mauve or deep pink. They decorated themselves with heavy silver ear-rings, toe-rings and anklets. The men wore cloth wound round their waists and through their legs with very long shirts over the top. They had either bare feet or sandals in plastic or leather. Some of the older girls wore European dress or Punjabi outfits, and the boys shorts. Many of the younger children were naked.

On one stretch of tree-lined road, we noticed a group of figures playing in the middle of the highway. We sounded our air-horns, and they scampered off the tarmac. To our amazement, they did not run into the fields, but leapt up into the trees with great agility. As we drove closer, we realised they were actually large baboons.

On reaching one river, we found that it was in flood, but it appeared that people were walking through the water easily. We therefore assayed to drive straight across, but the splashing of the water short-circuited our high tension system - and we came to a halt a little way into the flood.

"Don't worry!" came a voice from the shore. "We will get you through!"

At once a group of half a dozen Indian young men waded into the water, put their shoulders to the van, and pushed us right across the river onto dry ground.

While we waited for our electrical system to dry out, we thanked them and chatted about their lives and hopes. It always surprised us that these young people were so aware of world affairs and other cultures, despite being tucked away in places like this. We even had Indians enquiring how Manchester United had fared the previous Saturday!

Safe across the flooded river with willing manpower

Arriving in Jabulpur, we parked outside the railway station to investigate accommodation. There was nowhere to leave the van for a moment while Mike went to inquire. As I remained to guard the vehicle, faces were pressed against the windows - and when a chap started looking underneath, I press the air-horns loudly. The group melted away, and Mike came rushing out. There were people everywhere, sitting, sleeping, peering, leering, and engaged in other activities, judging by the smell.

Since Mike was not feeling too well, we decided to look for a good hotel. A friendly student on a bicycle recommended the Jackson Hotel, and escorted us to the entrance. It was very comfortable, and after having a delicious meal served in our room, we retired to bed. A good night's sleep seemed to put Mike right.

Meanwhile as we journeyed onward, I tried to keep up the project which I had begun at Dover, by writing a diary every day. With so many experiences and people along the way, it would have been easy to confuse the events when we subsequently looked back. Often the diarising was done on bumpy roads, but sometimes I found a quiet retreat in which to get up to date.

Hansard keeping the records

I began to wonder whether the continuous exposure to crowds of people, of unknown motives, was resulting in stress as we encountered these towns. Additionally, there was the constant anxiety about whether we would reach Madras in time to catch the ship that would take us into East Asia. These considerations put extra pressure on our need to keep travelling as fast as possible, and maybe were affecting our health.

****

Although our route was supposedly along the main artery of central India, its quality varied enormously. Much of the early part was on a beautiful forest road with a good surface and very little traffic. Monkeys with white fur and black faces played by the roadside. Huge herds of cattle plodded to new pastures, with their cowbells of wood or metal jangling merrily. This was greatly in contrast to the plains people, who had only one cow each or a small group of animals.

The road led through eucalyptus and teak plantations, and on rounding a corner we saw a peacock strutting proudly across in front of us.

In one village we stopped to investigate a film which was being shown in the open air. It was a coloured cartoon on the subject of family planning. Around the village, and in fact throughout the whole area, posters advocating family planning were pasted on walls and trees. Each showed a picture of parents with two children and proclaimed in Hindi the slogan "We are two - ours are two". There were hundreds of people watching the film show. Nearby stood a stage where a goddess sat woodenly staring at the people.

****

As we proceeded further south, the road deteriorated to poor quality asphalt. This was National Highway 7. Two hours out of Nagpur we came across a notice saying, "NH7 untrafficable through Hinganghat", and directing us via Chandra. We followed this diversion, and at one stage the road was so poor that a lorry ahead of us, which had pulled slightly to one side, was firmly stuck in the mud. Women were carrying stones in baskets on their heads to fill up the mud ruts and remedy the situation. Before long, the lorry was moved slightly, and we inched our way past. We followed a dusty road, and at one point passed an antique steamroller parked in the wilderness. Continuing on, we splashed through three fords, and negotiated a stretch of rough road which was in the process of being made up. Suddenly Mike had the feeling we were travelling in the wrong direction. Since our compass had been stolen in north India, and our maps did not show minor roads, we were really confused about what to do. We asked a couple of fellows the way to Rajura and they confirmed our suspicions. Turning around, we retraced the path, looking for a left turn and wracking our brains to try to remember a possible road. The steamroller attracted our attention again, and behind it a signpost in Hindi pointing out a muddy track. We inquired, and found that this track lead to Rajura. It was very bumpy in places but just dry enough for us to drive over. A new bridge at one point reassured us that one day in the future the road would be regarded as a major one. About a mile after we crossed the bridge, we encountered a stream. We splashed through, and found a village with a petrol station – this was Rajura, but probably did not appear on any maps. We inquired at the garage, and found a route to the Hyderabad road.

For most of the way we felt as though we were driving through an enormous country estate of forests and fields, despite this being apparently the main road to Hyderabad. At last, in the middle of a wooded area, we saw a sign "Welcome to Andra Pradesh", pointing towards Hyderabad. Seeing this written in English made us feel we were nearing the south of India.

In the middle of this park-like area, it was obvious that there was no suitable place to find accommodation. So, with some misgivings, we camped by the roadside in a little copse. It was a beautiful night and completely peaceful. But I cannot deny that I felt rather apprehensive, since we had been warned never to stop in central India at night in the countryside. Stories of outlaw dacoit bandits attacking lonely vehicles abounded – but, thankfully, we were undisturbed until the morning.

****

When we arrived at the Godavari River, we discovered that it had risen several feet above the roadway, because heavy rain in the hills behind had brought it up to flood level. We joined a queue of trucks and cars on the road leading down to the water, which was flowing very fast, and was about half a mile wide. Men were testing the depth by wading in, and it was obviously thigh-deep in places. A large truck decided to experiment and crawled through the water very slowly, often having difficulty keeping on the submerged road. Our dilemma was that this was the only crossing point of the Godavari for a long distance upstream or downstream. We studied the map for a while, and waited to see if other vehicles would succeed in crossing. In practice, we found nobody had the courage to risk being swept downstream in the cataract, and we concluded that our van would not stand much chance. The only possibility we could see from our maps was to drive upstream for 60 miles on a fairly poor road and cross at a town called Nirmal where there was apparently a bridge. Obviously it was possible that the crossing there was also under water. So, seeing no better alternative, we turned and started driving along the bank of the river in the upstream direction.

Very soon a tropical rainstorm hit us, and during the course of this the generator cut-out system failed. This meant that the battery was no longer charging, and that we could only run for a limited time before we had no power. Regretfully, we pulled to the side of the road, and I cooked lunch while Mike removed the cut-out system and inspected it. He found that a resistor in the electrical circuit had corroded and broken. Happily, before leaving London he had picked up a piece of scrap equipment which contained a similar component. Thus, he spent several hours, using a twelve-volt soldering iron, removing the resistor from the scrap mechanism and inserting it into our failed one. When refitted, the cut-out began to function again, although we did not know for how long it would last.

Just as we were about to leave after this excessive delay, Mike noticed that the back tyre was flat, and so a wheel-changing exercise had to take place.

Yet another challenge – yet another puncture

In the early evening, we drove into the outskirts of Nirmal, still not knowing whether the river was flooding too much for us to cross. Great was our rejoicing when we saw a high modern bridge over the river, and we quickly glided across it onto the far side.

We continued on along the road into the town of Nizamabad, arriving very late at night. Again we stopped near to the railway station to look for accommodation, but we found that the whole area was covered with literally hundreds of people sleeping in and around the station. I had a strange sensation in that place, and felt distinctly uncomfortable with the atmosphere. The people seemed to be totally inert, but all staring into space in a strange way. Some folk were eyeing us in a manner that was hard to describe. Mike named the place as "The International Headquarters for Leerers and Peerers". Even he, who is not usually so sensitive to spiritual atmospheres, said he felt that there was an evil presence in that area. In view of our disquiet, we drove out of the city and parked on the outskirts - near enough to the town to avoid bandits, but far enough to avoid the unpleasant population.

****

The events of the last week had been really wearying and frustrating, although our minds were filled with interesting images that we would not quickly forget. As we drove towards Hyderabad, we decided to look for some rather more luxurious accommodation for the next night. A guidebook recommended a hotel built on a hillside covered with strange rocky outcrops. The legend was that the Creator threw down all the surplus building materials from creation into this area. Thus we were delighted to drive through the gates of the Rock Castle Hotel, and find that we could rent a small suite with a magnificent view over the city of Hyderabad. The hotel itself reeked of colonial opulence, although to some extent tarnished. It was designed as a whitewashed castle, with a staff dressed in uniforms which would have been fashionable a century before. Meals were served on a patio with an amazing vista of south India, and the food was good. Staying at the hotel was a large group of people attending an international ophthalmology conference. We had interesting conversations with several of the delegates, particularly one American lady with a vast experience of treating eye complaints in tropical countries.

****

We left our castle at 6 am, considerably refreshed after a spectacular time perched on the heights, and anxious to head for the coast. The hotel had provided us with packed breakfasts, and we descended into the city of Hyderabad, where we bought bread and sitaphul, a cone-shaped fruit, in the early morning light. The cities of south India were different from the north in many ways, one of which was the proliferation of Hindu temples adorned with porcelain statues of the gods on their roofs.

Highly decorated Hindu temple in south India

Soon our road passed through open, undulating country, well cultivated despite the huge rocks protruding from the landscape. We dropped from over 2000 feet down to sea level. It was just as well that we were travelling mainly downhill, as we could only scrape together 17 rupees for petrol, and knew that our US dollars would not be accepted in the countryside. However, we had seven gallons of fuel on the roof, and worked out that it should be just enough. Passing through places with such intriguing names as Chitoor, Vellore and Poonamallee, we eventually found ourselves coming into Madras. Soon we realised what a vast metropolis this port city was. From a guidebook we had chosen the Claridges Hotel as being suitable in price and position for us. After experiencing a few Hindglish-speaking people, we were directed to the hotel by a garage attendant. We checked in, and found that the service was poor, but that the food was excellent. After dinner, we planned to walk to the sea. However, the stench of stale urine pervaded the streets to such an extent that we were forced to cancel our ramble, and retraced our steps.

On arrival at the port, we found that we had a few days to spare before the departure of the ship. This was a good thing, because the following day was a half holiday, the day after was a public holiday in celebration of Nasser's death in Egypt, and the next one was a religious holiday! Also, during those three days Mike was unwell with a sinus and ear infection, and so stayed in bed in the hotel. Dr Margaret had given me a prescription for penicillin, to be used in eventualities such as this, and I went in search of a trustworthy pharmacy. After a few doses Mike felt better, and was soon back in action again.

****

On the next working day, we went to the offices of Binnie & Co, the agents for the shipping line. Our bookings were confirmed, and the clerk explained that we would need to complete the necessary formalities before boarding. We were quite prepared to fill in a few forms, but the man said, with a sly smile, that there was a handling agent in the waiting room outside who could do the work for us. The man was to be trusted he assured us. Feeling confident that we could manage without assistance, we did, however, go and talk to the little man waiting outside. He was small and dark, with a pair of gold-rimmed spectacles perched on his nose, and carried a suitcase bulging with paper.

"Good morning, Sir and Madam. My name is Prasad. I trust that you are well."

"Very well, thank you, Mr Prasad. We are shipping our car on the Rajula…"

"Yes, indeed. I assume that you are Mr Collier with a Bedford CA van."

"You seem very well informed."

"It is my job," he replied, with a deprecating smile. "If it is your desire, I will be honoured to act as your handling agent, sir."

"Well, er… what would it cost?"

"I will take care of the whole process for a fee of 200 rupees."

"200 rupees? And what would that involve?" I exclaimed.

"It is a considerably very extremely complicated business – and I have had the privilege of serving many foreigners in your position before."

"Of course, of course. But what would be the procedure?"

"First you need to complete arrangements to re-export your vehicle from India."

"What does that mean?"

"Initially, it must be weighed and inspected. This takes place at a weighbridge in the lower docks area."

At this point he produced a large map of Madras, and with his finger traced a course through back-streets, which made Hampton Court maze seem like child's play.

"Then what?" enquired Mike hesitantly.

"Your documents must be verified at an office here," he said, indicating a location on the edge of the map.

The smiling little man continued, "After that, your vehicle will pass through customs, then obtain port clearance. That will permit me to start the procedure for transferring it to the shipping line. Finally, you can drive to the relevant quay on the day before sailing - and loading will take place."

We looked rather nonplussed after this recital. But he pressed his point, by producing from his case a sheaf of papers.

"These are the forms you need to fill in. Unfortunately, in India the bureaucracy is quite convoluted. Each form must be written in sextuplicate."

"What does that mean?"

"Simply that there are six copies of each form." was the smiling rejoinder.

"And you would do all of these things for 200 rupees?"

"Certainly. It would be my pleasure."

We looked at each other – and simultaneously nodded and capitulated.

"Mr Prasad, we would be happy to employ you as our agent."

The man proved to be excellent, guiding us through the labyrinth of Madras to a weighbridge, and then to various offices. It was obvious that, being well-known in these places, he was able to lubricate the processes considerably.

On the day prior to sailing, we drove down to the dockside, and parked on the quay next to the ship. Slings were placed around the van, and a giant derrick swung over the side of the vessel, picked up our puny vehicle, and dropped it into one of the cavernous holds on board.

Loading time on the Madras dock

The next morning we presented ourselves at the port immigration offices. There was some confusion over the cash that we wanted to take out of the country, since receipts were required for all that we had spent in India. Eventually this was overcome by Mike making a hasty taxi ride back to Claridges Hotel, where he obtained a receipt which satisfied the officials. After passing through a medical check, police check and the customs section, we walked up the gangplank onto the ship.

During all this process we had been expecting to see our handling agent. At one point, Mr Prasad had taken our passports for one final stage of processing. Now standing on the deck of the ship, we realised that he was nowhere in sight. We looked down hopefully at the dock, expecting to see our man and our documents. We wondered what we would be the outcome if we arrived in Malaysia with no passports. Suddenly the ship's hooter gave a loud blast, and we saw men on the shore scrabbling to untie the warps from the ship. Still no sign of our agent! Then, to our dismay the first and second of the gangways to the ship were drawn back, and we saw men pulling on the ropes to remove the third gangway, breaking us from contact with the land forever.

Just at that moment, we saw a small figure sprinting through the people on the quay, reaching the foot of the gangway as it began to move, hurtling up the steps and onto the ship, just before it separated. With relief, we recognised our trustworthy agent!

Soon Mr Prasad appeared beside us with big smiles and two passports.

"Well - you only just made it!" Mike said.

"I've done this many times," laughed the agent.

"But how will you get off?" I asked him. "Or are you coming all the way to Malaysia with us?"

"Not at all!" he said. "I will go back with the pilot on his little boat."

Gradually Madras faded into a smoky haze in the distance. We looked back with excitement on the stimulating experiences we had found in India - an enormous kaleidoscope of people and places in this ancient land.

Chapter 12
Rajula

As the ship was being piloted down the Cooum River from Madras, we went to look for our berths. Before leaving Britain, we had been informed by the P & O office that the ship's accommodation was almost full, and they could only offer us berths in separate cabins with five other people of the same gender. Thus we went below, and I found my bed in a fairly small, internal cabin shared with five other girls, while Mike went to locate his berth in another part of the ship. Not long afterwards, conversing with my new cabin mates, I heard one say that there were plenty of empty rooms on the ship. Apparently, she had heard the purser mention this.

Immediately I found Mike, and together we went to the purser, who was an avuncular, elderly English gentleman of the old school.

"Good afternoon," we said. "We have heard a rumour that there may be some spare accommodation on the ship – we are at present in separate cabins."

"Well, actually, since you mention it, we have quite a few spare spaces," he replied. "Let me see your tickets."

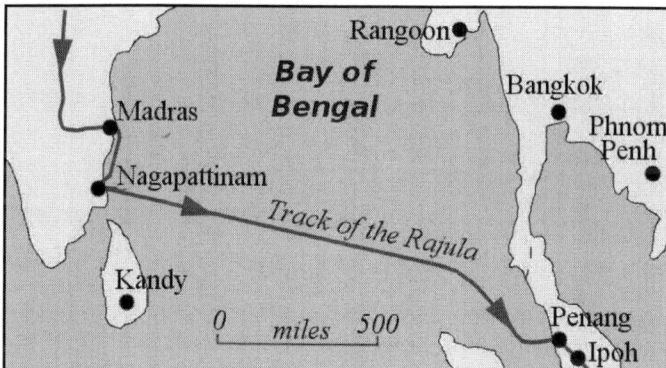

After studying the papers for a moment, he offered, "I do have a double cabin available. It's an outside one with a porthole. But it's a bit more expensive I'm afraid."

"Well, we'll certainly take it. Anything to be together for the next seven days!"

"Very well. I will send the attendant down to show you the way."

"But they told us in London that the ship was full!"

"Those fools in Britain always mess up the booking arrangements. We have this problem every month. And we are losing money because of it."

As we were leaving his office, the purser called out, "By the way if you take that cabin, then you won't eat in the main dining room. Your meals will be at the captain's table."

And so we moved into a small, cosy, little cabin, having two bunks one above the other, a small wash basin, a tiny cupboard, and a large porthole looking straight out across the ocean. When dinner-time came, a steward showed us the way to the captain's dining room, where we joined a dozen other people around a large table.

The captain himself was a fairly gruff old man, who had sailed this route times beyond number, and was about to retire. He seemed rather miffed with having to entertain young adventurers, rather than the gentry of fifty years before. In contrast, the younger officers were much more interesting. The chief engineer was a red-headed Scotsman, full of vitality, wit and anecdotes. We took to him immediately, and he enlivened our seven days of repasts on board the Rajula.

From these folk we learned that the ship was carrying 1800 Indian labourers, who were going to Malaysia on contract to work on the rubber plantations. When we expressed surprise, the officers told us that the Indians had boarded the ship by a separate low-level entrance, and that they were confined to two decks below the level of our

- 160 -

accommodation. It all seemed very class conscious and colonial. Following an excellent meal, we retired to our little refuge and had a good night's sleep.

At dawn, Mike suddenly shouted from the top bunk.

"Look out of the porthole. There's an Indian dhow!"

And sure enough, I saw a lateen-rigged sailing vessel framed in the circular window.

Dhow ahoy!

But when we went up on deck, we discovered this craft was not alone. Scores of such dhows were sailing towards the ship – and if we had not known better we might have thought we were under pirate attack. At the same time we noticed that the ship's engines had stopped, and that we were rolling gently on the swell. We asked a passing officer what was going on.

"Every trip, we stop at Nagapattinam, just down the Indian coast," he explained. "We load a cargo of onions from south India which are shipped across to Malaysia.".

As we watched, the dhows sailed up to the side of the ship and moored. Stevedores scrambled aboard, the hatch covers on the decks were removed, and the derricks sent their hooks reaching down into the dhows.

Many tons of onions going into the same hold as our van

The onions were packed in large wicker baskets which were piled into huge nets on the little boats, and were then lifted by the ship's cranes into the holds.

With concern, we peered down into the hold where our van had been placed, and saw that a heavy plank floor had been laid across, above our vehicle. Hundreds of tons of onions were being loaded on top. We wondered how our camper would smell after a week in that environment! The loading operation took nearly the whole day, accompanied by incessant shouting from the crew, labourers and dhow skippers. Towards evening the job was finished, and we heard the engines restart. Slowly the lights of south India receded astern.

****

The next few days continued without much variety, but we were really glad of the respite from continual concern about roads and vehicle repairs. We spent some time each day chatting to the other passengers and reading a number of books. There was a fair spread of nationalities on board, being predominantly Indian, but including people from other parts of Asia travelling to Singapore. One kind man offered to sell us some rolls of colour film, since we had been unable to buy any in India. For three days, the boat was rolling too much to make reading easy, and the delicious meals were not enjoyed to their full, because of the perpetual discomfort of the stomach. Overall, we enjoyed the seven-day trip, and found that little things each day added to the general routine of life on board. We found some Scrabble addicts among the passengers. On some evenings there were cocktails with the captain, where we learned quite a bit about the ship from the officers. They said that the Rajula was launched in 1926 in Scotland, and was 477 feet in length at the water line.

On two evenings there were film-shows in the main saloon, one being a documentary on British India – no doubt very politically correct on that particular ship! On another evening, we saw "The Impossible Years", an American film about a family with two teenage girls. Sitting in the middle of the Indian Ocean, we felt about as remote as could be from the culture of that film.

We asked one of the officers if we could see what conditions were like for the less fortunate passengers living below us. He took us down a staircase and showed us two decks reserved for the Indian labourers and their families. Apparently, Europeans were forbidden to travel on these two levels, although one cannot imagine voluntarily choosing to do so. The upper level of the two contained simple wooden bunks fixed in rows across the deck, while the lower level was one enormous floor divided by white lines into squares which delineated the living space for each family. Obviously, visions of slave ships rose in our minds when we saw these conditions, but we reminded ourselves that these people did consider it worthwhile to make this journey across the Bay of Bengal.

Mike had befriended the chief engineer, who invited him to visit the engine room. The equipment in the roaring cacophony of the semi-darkness was in excellent shiny condition. The engine itself was one of the first oil-fired reciprocating steam engines, boasting eight enormous cylinders, driving a pair of huge propellers. At full power the ship could make a speed of about 13 knots.

On the fifth evening, following dinner, the captain invited us onto the bridge. We had a marvellous view of the sunset in the west, but looking in the opposite direction towards our destination we could see nothing but empty sea. Then the captain called us over to the radar screen, where we could make out the northern end of Sumatra. The next day we saw a Japanese fishing vessel out of Penang, which was the first sighting on the voyage so far.

Although our journey would take us to Singapore, we had decided to leave the ship at Penang, so that we could drive down the length of Peninsular Malaysia, after which we would cross the causeway to Singapore island as the grand finale.

****

Most of the passengers were on deck early on the final morning, straining through binoculars for a first view of Malaysia. Just after sunrise, a beautiful rainbow appeared ahead with the black sails of a junk silhouetted against it.

Slowly we watched the island of Penang come closer and closer. Wooded hills stood behind little villages clustered on the narrow coastal strip. In the calm clear water, we could see jellyfish gliding just below the surface.

The harbour of Penang looked very crowded with ships large and small. We anchored well offshore, and waited for several hours. At last, a small boat was seen speeding towards us, bearing on its side the word "Immigration". The launch drew up to the gangway, and smartly dressed Chinese immigration officials climbed swiftly aboard. They set up an office in the saloon, and one by one passengers were processed with great efficiency, until all the necessary procedures were completed.

In the late afternoon, Rajula began to move again, and eventually pulled alongside a wharf right next to the town. Before long, we had collected our luggage and disembarked.

The first impression of Penang was that it was so clean and modern. There were pavements and kerbs at the roadside, beautiful shops, lovely buildings, and yet a touch of the east in the rickshaws and markets.

We were invited to spend the weekend with an English couple who were working in Penang. The next morning we attended a service in St Paul's Church, where the congregation was mainly English-speaking Chinese, most of whom were young people.

Returning to the harbour, we found that the vehicle had already been unloaded from underneath the onions, and was standing parked on the quayside. However, when we tried to start, we found that the brakes had locked completely - no doubt from close proximity to several tons of damp onions for a week. So Mike started his life in East Asia by crawling under the van with spanners and readjusting the brakes, until the vehicle was mobile again.

****

After lunch we travelled out to the famous Snake Temple of Penang. As we headed towards the place, we had vivid pictures of what the inside of this strange place of worship would be like. We had been told that the snakes were venomous and quite ubiquitous inside the building. But, on arrival we found it rather disappointing. The temple itself was not very large, and inside the sanctuary the poisonous vipers seemed to be completely drugged by the multitude of burning joss-sticks.

Sleepy pit vipers greeted us in the Snake Temple

In truth, the reptiles were everywhere, hanging from ornaments, branches and lights – but we did not find sleepy snakes too threatening. Unexpectedly, I felt that the baby snakes were really rather sweet. Outside the front entrance, there were two defanged vipers for people to handle. This temple was built for a Chinese deity Chor Soo Kong. It began as a simple attap house, but as the power of the deity grew, a more solid temple was constructed in 1873.

We had been recommended to visit the peak of Penang Hill, and so caught a bus to the funicular railway station. After sampling a delicious fried banana from a roadside stall, we entered the car for the ride up the hill. The track rose steeply through thick undergrowth, past huge boulders and attractive jungle flowers - with glimpses of flimsy bungalows hidden in the trees. As the car glided higher, we could see Georgetown below us, and across the straits Butterworth on the mainland of Malaysia. We found that the highest point of Penang Hill was about 10°C cooler than the coast, being 2723 feet above sea level. The island had been the scene of many colonial battles, as Britain, Holland and Portugal struggled for supremacy in the area. A lone cannon on the summit spoke of the turbulent history of these straits.

A cannon on Penang Hill reminded us of former struggles

In the summit restaurant we enjoyed a meal of baked crab, followed by rice, chop suey and sweet and sour pork. An ice cream and coffee completed the dinner. We watched the Rajula steaming slowly out of the harbour, and then gazed at the sunset as night fell on the town below. Gradually all the lights were switched on and we saw a mass of twinkling colours.

Chapter 13
Rubber Time

The next morning Mike went through the procedure of visiting various government offices, in order to free the van from the Penang docks. Although it took quite a while, the officials were polite and cooperative at every stage. Eventually he emerged with the release permit for us to drive officially into Malaysia.

While he was handling the paperwork, I borrowed a bicycle from our hosts, and cycled around the town looking for vegetables. At one market, I was accosted by two young lads who were charging 10 cents for cycle parking. From previous experience, I assumed they were simply trying to make a quick buck without any real authority.

Subsequently, when I came out with my purchases, my bicycle was hemmed in. The boys produced a permit, written in English and Malay, showing that they had official sanction for the parking charge. After reading this, I paid up.

Next, we made time to clean out the vehicle, ridding ourselves of many kilograms of Central Asian dust, and then joined the ferry queue to cross the short stretch of water from Penang Island to the mainland. A twenty-minute ride on the packed car ferry brought us to the town of Butterworth on the peninsula part of Malaysia. There were no customs problems as we disembarked – and no road-signs either! So we followed the main road, and soon found that we were on the highway for Kuala Lumpur.

The scenery was radically different from previous countries, comprising dense green tropical forests on steep hillsides. Everything looked damp and fertile, and the hot atmosphere was extremely humid. The leaves on many of the trees were large, thick and rubbery, of a dark green colour.

We noticed a terrific increase in traffic compared with recent weeks, and were rather disconcerted by the extremely fast driving. Techniques were quite different from our previous experiences, since the well-surfaced road was almost always of the three-lane variety. Malaysian drivers seem to enjoy a dangerous game of "Chicken!". When a car decided to overtake, it pulled into the middle lane, flashing its headlights vigorously, and sped straight along. At that moment a car coming the opposite way might do exactly the same, threatening with its lights. We were amazed how close two cars would come before one of them suddenly swerved back into the inner lane. Nevertheless, we saw evidence of several serious pile-ups by the roadside.

We spent the first night parked at a petrol station at Chemor, and were very relieved to find the Chinese so polite and willing to converse intelligently with us. It seemed that most of the administrative positions in the country were held by Chinese, while lower-level operatives were normally Malays. There seemed to be some friction between the two races, and in order to rectify the imbalance, the Malaysian government had brought in a rule that all companies must have at least one Malay board member in place.

It appeared that the major difference lay in work ethic, with the Chinese restlessly active, and the Malays taking a more relaxed view of life. It was joked that the latter culture did not pay much attention to deadlines or schedules – operating on "rubber time"!

****

We left Chemor, and then passed through the district centre of Ipoh. Everywhere was clean and smart. For long distances we were travelling through endless forests of rubber trees. These plantations were the basis of Malaysia's wealth, and had been the reason for the British occupation in colonial days. It seemed to us that the whole process of extraction was highly labour intensive, as the little cups had to be positioned and then emptied frequently on each of many thousands of trees. Obviously, the global demand for rubber made it worthwhile for the country to continue this industry.

We were rather embarrassed to learn that originally Brazil was the main rubber producer – but that in 1876 a British businessman smuggled seeds out of Amazonia to the Botanical Gardens in London. After grafting, the seeds became the basis of the vast rubber plantations in British Malaya. The trees were planted only 4 metres apart, unlike their South American counterparts which might be several miles distant from each other in the jungle. This gave the Asian plantations a distinct edge, which resulted in the demise of the Brazilian industry.

Latex-producers dripping quietly

The road then took us on to Tapah, where Mike characteristically made some feeble comments about "rubber Tapahs". By this time the bumper bracket on the front of the van had fractured again, and so we stopped at a Chinese garage to have the offender welded back. The job was done very speedily, and then to our surprise the lads did not charge us for the work.

In many of the villages we saw badminton courts marked out under the trees. Several times, while travelling in the evening, we saw games in progress under floodlights. It seemed that this was the national game, being ideally suited to the calm nights in the forests.

The Malay language fascinated us, as we looked at the various notices and signs along our journey. A local young man explained that the roots of Malay stretched back two thousand years, but that over the centuries it had absorbed a large number of words from Arabic and

Persian, together with modern terms in the last hundred years. One interesting feature was that plurals were denoted by repeating of the same word. Thus "man" was "orang", but "men" would be "orang orang".

This made some written sentences excessively long, and so a convention had developed in which the mathematical squared sign was used. So "men" would appear on signs as "orang^2". Needless to say, this made some signs look very funny to the English reader!

****

One of our guidebooks stated that the general geography of the Malay peninsula was fairly simple. A central spine of high mountains ran down its length, with broad coastal plains on either side and to the south.

Most of the population lived on the lowland areas, since they were well-watered by rivers flowing off the central massif. The uplands were rugged areas of very dense tropical rainforest, which provided the habitat for the orangutan, literally "man-of-the-forest".

It was our intention to visit these central mountains of Malaysia, and so we turned off the main north-south route at Tapah. The narrow winding road quickly began to climb.

In many ways it reminded us of Nepal, but the vegetation at the roadsides was much thicker and more luscious. The good surface was continually marred by landslides of red, sticky mud caused by the heavy rains – but we slithered through these obstacles without serious incident.

At last we reached Tanah Rata, whose name means a flat place, well describing this little plateau among the high hills. It was a small town, surrounded by jungle, in which we saw a number of typical Malay villages, known as "kampongs".

A kampong in the forests of Malaysia

From there we continued up into the central area of the Cameron Highlands. At one point a road sign announced "One way road ahead". Coming round a bend, we found a large "Stop!" sign before us, and two cars waiting. A notice informed us that the road ahead was so steep, narrow and dangerous that it could only be used by traffic in one direction at a time, with each way allowed one hour. We wandered over to a small sentry box, where a young Malay man told us that it would be half an hour before we could go up. Soon cars began to descend, indicating that it must be quite a long stretch of one-way road. Then we heard the jangling of a telephone bell, and noticed a wire running up through the trees beside the road ahead. After confirming that all the traffic had come down, the watchman reversed his "Stop!" sign so that we could start up the incline. The trackway was very narrow, and at times we had thick undergrowth brushing one side of the van. I drove slowly round the twisting bends as we went higher and higher up the mountainside, with incredible views across the huge wooded valleys. Mike kept watch on the other side, where a steep drop into dense jungle terrified us. Finally, we came out of this section, passing another sentry box where a short line of cars was waiting to descend.

It was our intention to visit a school in the Cameron Highlands, where we had an introduction, and could camp for a couple of days. After much searching along leafy roads, we found a relevant sign, and then drove through a beautiful country lane, reminiscent of England. The school was set in a clearing in the jungle, and was a modern building surrounded by beautiful grounds. We were welcomed, and invited to camp in the vehicle on the edge of the school playing fields. Chefoo School had a multicultural population of students, ranging from primary to upper secondary level. It had been founded mainly to provide education for the children of people working in Malaysia and surrounding nations, who could not find ample educational opportunities locally. There was a lovely atmosphere in the school, and we were invited to dine with several members of staff, and even provided with the luxury of a hot bath!

Chefoo School, Cameron Highlands

We slept in the van at night, but found that we needed a sleeping bag for the first time in many weeks. The air was cold, which was not surprising at 6000 feet above sea level. Next morning we had breakfast outside the van, and were visited by the school's pet monkey who joined us. He was particularly pleased with the banana that we gave him, and he chewed away happily.

We donned our old clothes and walking boots, and set off for a jungle walk to a local peak. The school staff warned us about a few things.

"Be very careful to follow the way markers on the track," one of them advised. "We've had cases of people wandering a few metres into the jungle, and never coming out. You lose your sense of direction so quickly in there."

"Right - we'll try and stay on the straight and narrow," quipped Mike.

"Also keep a watch out for snakes – possibly asleep on the path."

"Any other dangers?" I asked.

"Actually, the most dangerous are the hornet swarms. They can quickly kill a person. In fact, our children at the school are trained to fall flat on their faces in the jungle whenever they hear a shout of "Down!". Hornets will fly over you - but attack if you are standing up."

So, suitably briefed, we clambered up the steep tracks through the tropical forest which enveloped the mountains. Streams of water trickled down the path, not finding alternative courses in the dense undergrowth. After an hour's hot climbing, we arrived at the summit of Mount Jesar. A shelter had been erected in the clearing on the top, from which a magnificent view stretched east to Tanah Rata and west towards the coastal plain - and south into our lunch bags! The jungle track, marked periodically with small numbers, wound its way back down the hillside to the road south of the town, and from there we returned to the school. Happily, neither snakes nor hornets had been encountered!

Arriving just in time for tea at the school's "holiday bungalow", a beautiful mansion at the head of a valley, we spent another enjoyable evening with some of the staff. Supper was terrific, despite the missing pineapple stolen by the pet monkey. Quite incongruously, after the meal, we watched a showing of the film "Jungle Cat", while we nibbled popcorn made by a Canadian member of staff.

On our last morning at Chefoo, we were asked if we would take one of the children down to a village where the rest of his class was enjoying a half-term outing by a lake. Following the same road down through the hills, descending the one-way section carefully, we dropped our little charge with his classmates, and then made our way down to Tapah. A man by the roadside with a punctured tyre needed a lift, and so we took him to the town.

****

Back on the main north-south highway, we sped on past Kuala Lumpur on a fast motorway. Having discovered that there were virtually no camping facilities, we turned off the highway towards Malacca. We had been given the address of mutual friends there, and were hoping to park for the night outside their house. In the event, they were more than welcoming, inviting us to dinner, and then letting us sleep in the van on their property. However, it had taken quite a while to find their place, since house numbers were not consecutive, but followed the building order along each road.

Next morning we toured Malacca which had a long and turbulent history. According to our friends, it had been a thriving port around 1400 AD under its first Sultan. Even the enormous Chinese fleet of Zheng He had stopped here for a long period. In the 1500s the Portuguese seized the town, and controlled trade through the Straits. A century later, the Dutch conquered the place, and used it as a way-station for ships sailing to the East Indies. Yet another hundred years later, an Anglo-Dutch treaty saw Malacca become British territory. Ruled at first by the British East India Company, it then became a crown colony, and later was amalgamated into the Straits Settlements, together with Singapore and Penang. At the termination of British rule, it became a major port and state of independent Malaysia.

Our explorations of the city were curtailed by a severe tropical rainstorm. Within minutes, the roads were flooded, but the deep drains on each side coped well - so that as soon as the rain ceased the water abated.

Steep-roofed Malay houses on stilts

We left Malacca, following the coastal road beside the straits, but there was marshland between us and the actual seafront. The road ran through Malay kampongs, made up of the steep roofed houses also found in Indonesia. We learned that Chinese villages were built with houses of brick standing on the ground, while Malay dwellings were always of wood raised on stilts.

Following the coastline, we turned eastward into the large city of Johore Bahru. Seeing no road-signs, we drove on through the suburbs, and began to feel that we were hopelessly lost. Without much idea of where we were going, we found that we had joined a very fast motorway, and yet had no clue in which direction it was heading.

Suddenly Mike shouted, "Look – there's water on both sides of us. This must be the causeway to Singapore island!"

Chapter 14
Lion City

Our dramatic entry into Singapore, after thousands of miles on the road, was not as glorious as we had expected. The immigration officers at the end of the causeway regarded us with suspicion, and seemed loath to let us into their island kingdom.

"Where have you come from? Why is there no one here to meet you? Where will you go from here?"

We endured a grilling for a considerable while. From this, we inferred that Singapore was not keen to welcome young people from the West. It seemed they were afraid of hippies, who might bring drugs and disease into the country. Thus they searched our vehicle and checked our documents thoroughly. One of our interrogators then left the group, and went into an office. Through a window we could see him talking animatedly into a phone. We guessed he was asking for instructions from a higher authority regarding a couple in a battered van who claimed to have come from London.

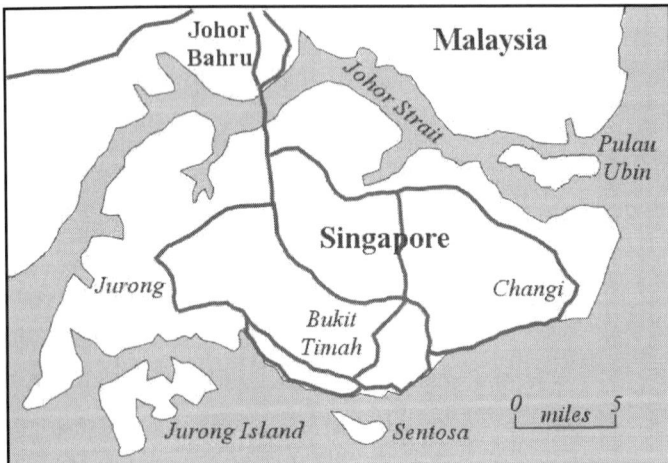

Previously we had heard that Singapore took a dim view of foreigners with long locks, and so we had taken the precaution of having haircuts a few days before. Nevertheless, the officials at the border took a long time ascertaining that we were not going to corrupt the strict principles of the island state. Half an hour later, the Chinese officer came out to the desk. We assumed that he had received his instructions regarding us.

"You may give them temporary visas," he ordered the clerk, "and temporary import for their vehicle."

Thus we belatedly entered the Republic of Singapore.

Short back-and-sides haircuts were de rigueur for foreigners

Immediately after leaving the frontier, we found ourselves on an oriental version of the Brands Hatch racing circuit. Locked in the middle of a mass of high speed traffic, we scanned the road-signs for the area to which we were going. Suddenly we recognised among the mass of brightly-lit blue signs the words "Bukit Timah", and quickly exited from the crowded motorway. Happily, our sparse directions proved adequate, and before long we turned into the spacious grounds of the language school where we were expected.

At once we were welcomed by the staff, and settled into a comfortable room. It was extremely hot and very humid, making us glad that the building had a modern air-conditioning system.

****

The next morning we began to explore Singapore, finding it ultra-clean, as a result of the tight litter laws. The area of Bukit Timah was in the central part of the metropolis, and provided a great range of shops and department stores. Together with other young people of various nationalities who would be studying languages with us, we discovered the delights of Orchard Road, where we could eat satay to our hearts content in little Malay restaurants. This was the traditional food of barbequed, skewered meat served with a peanut sauce. In the same area were Chinese and Indian eating-places, all offering authentic homeland dishes.

After looking at the milometer on the van, Mike decided that Singapore needed an additional road sign – and so nailed his own creation to a tree, signifying the thirteen weeks and six hundred gallons of petrol that lay between us and our departure from London.

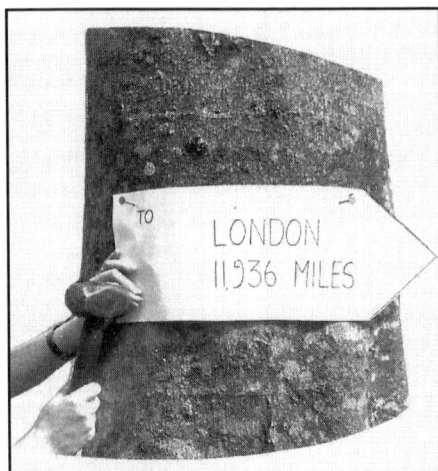

****

Our reason for booking into this language school was that both of us wanted to be involved in education in the Chinese world. Seeing that mainland China was closed at that time, we opted for Hong Kong. In preparation for moving there, we had decided to take a language course in Cantonese Chinese. Over the next few weeks, we sat for many hours in a language laboratory, or had small group sessions with Chinese teachers. For us it was a completely new experience to tackle a tonal Asian tongue – totally unlike the languages of western Europe. Cantonese was a particular challenge, in that each sound could have one of seven different meanings depending on the intonation with which it was spoken. Added to this, was the fact of Chinese characters being non-phonetic, and requiring hours of memorisation to fix their meanings and sounds in our heads. However, we thoroughly enjoyed the time and the people in the language school, and felt after three months, that we were beginning to make some progress.

****

I asked the director of the institution about the history of Singapore, and he gave me a very concise summary of what was obviously a very complicated story.

"The myth goes like this. During the 13th Century a prince of the empire of Shrivijaya landed on this island. The first thing he saw was a lion, which he took as an auspicious sign, from which he proceeded to found a settlement here. He named it Singapura, meaning "lion city" in Malay. The island became an important trading port during the Malacca Sultanate and the turbulent centuries that followed. Eventually in 1818, Sir Stamford Raffles agreed with the Sultan of Johore to establish a trading post - and modern Singapore was born as a British colony. Although the Japanese occupied the islands during WWII, it reverted to British rule afterwards. When independence came to Malaya, Singapore became part of the new Malaysia. Owing to racial tensions, Singapore was expelled in 1965, and became an independent nation state."

****

Other fascinating information about the place was gleaned by observation. For example, we soon worked out that the weather pattern was remarkably consistent – vastly different from that of Britain. Each day began with clear skies and slowly increasing temperature. Round about midday, clouds would form, and then 2 o'clock would see the beginning of an enormous downpour. The streets would flood almost immediately, and the water pour off into the wide drains on each side. After two hours the deluge would slacken and cease, followed by the return of the sun. This would cause instant evaporation, with steam rising off the roads, and resulting in an unpleasantly high blanket of humidity. This may have been the background to the two-hour siesta which was observed throughout the city.

Furthermore, the location of Singapore almost on the equator resulted in day and night being of equal length throughout the year. This, together with the predictable weather, made the days all very similar – very different from the British climate with its short winter days and long summer evenings.

****

Singapore island had a variety of areas. In the north part we saw kampongs, similar to those in Malaysia, while the south fringe constituted a well-developed business district of high-rise buildings, fronting onto the harbour around the prestigious Raffles Hotel. To the west in Jurong, an industrial area was expanding rapidly, and much of the centre of the island was covered with residential areas in a booming expansion of construction work.

A place of rather morbid historical interest that we visited was Changi, the site of the infamous prison camp where the Japanese interned a large number of British personnel in WWII. The camp itself had been destroyed, and the area was desolate – and we heard rumours that an airport might be built there in the future.

One evening we decided to visit the Botanical Gardens after dark. Such excursions in Singapore were quite safe, owing to the high level of policing everywhere. It was extremely pleasant walking along the well-lit paths through the varied trees, shrubs and flowers. But when we strayed off the path into the dark areas, we found that there were entwined couples almost everywhere. Finally, we deduced that in the strict moral atmosphere of Singapore it was difficult for boys and girls to meet openly, and that the gardens provided a secluded environment for such amorous encounters!

****

讀萬卷書 行萬里路

At the end of one of the Chinese language sessions, a teacher approached me with a sheet of paper in her hand, saying, "Pam, I've been thinking about your journey. I've written out a Chinese proverb which seems to suit you well."

"Thank you, very much," I replied, taking the sheet and seeing eight Chinese characters, only two of which I recognised! "Can you tell me the translation?"

"It says: 'To travel ten thousand miles is better than reading ten thousand books'."

After thanking her, I began to ponder its meaning, and concluded that what we had experienced over the last thirteen weeks was infinitely superior to anything we could have obtained simply by study.

I thought of all the wonderful people we had met...

    ...the Greeks who pulled us out of the sand,

    ...the generous Turkish farm-hands,

    ...Nurettin on Mount Olympus,

    ...Dr Jock and Dr Margaret serving in their hospitals,

    ...our gracious hosts in Lahore,

    ...friendly students in India,

    ...the Tenaja family,

    ...and the dedicated people at Chefoo School.

All of them, and many others, had enriched our lives in some way. If we had flown by air straight to Singapore, we would have missed the rich tapestry of humanity which had stretched along our route. Having seen so many people struggling to survive in tough environments, we were made more acutely aware of the privileges that we enjoyed.

In terms of places, we were also grateful for the opportunity to see at first hand the spectrum of cities with amazing buildings, towns, villages, rivers, deserts and lakes that had passed before our eyes.

We both realised that in some ways the last three months had changed us as people – had given us a new perspective on the world, its needs and wonders. With such thoughts we looked to the future, whatever that might hold.

Chapter 15
Chronology of the Trip

Our journey lasted from July 15th to October 16th 1970, covering 11,936 miles, through fourteen countries. The van consumed 600 gallons of petrol – and an immeasurable amount of engine oil! The whole trip took 94 days.

Day 1	London to Aachen in GERMANY
Day 2	To Basle in SWITZERLAND
Day 3	To Brunnen
Day 4	To Bellinzona in ITALY
Day 5	Camped at Bellinzonza
Day 6	To Venice
Day 7	To Pesaro
Day 8	To Pescara
Day 9	To Bari
Day 10	To Brindisi; overnight ferry to GREECE
Day 11	To Patras
Day 12	Camped at Patras
Day 13	To Corinth
Day 14	To Olympus Beach Campsite
Day 15	To Kavalla
Day 16	To Istanbul in TURKEY
Day 17	Explored Istanbul
Day 18	To Bursa
Day 19	Ascended Mount Olympus near Bursa
Day 20	To Akhisar
Day 21	To Alasehir
Day 22	To Ephesus
Day 23	To Isparta

Day 24	To Manargat
Day 25	To Silifke Mocamp
Day 26	Camped at Silifke
Day 27	To Adana
Day 28	To Urfa
Day 29	To breakdown near Maden
Day 30	To Bingol
Day 31	To Malazgirt
Day 32	To Dogubayazit
Day 33	Day of rest below Ararat
Day 34	To Tabriz in IRAN
Day 35	Explored Tabriz
Day 36	To Teheran
Day 37	To Behshahr
Day 38	To desert road near Caspian Sea
Day 39	To battery failure outside Ghoochan
Day 40	To Meshed
Day 41	To Taiebad
Day 42	To desert road in AFGHANISTAN
Day 43	To Kandahar
Day 44	To Ghazni
Day 45	To Kabul
Day 46	Stayed at NOOR Hospital, Kabul
Day 47	Explored Kabul
Day 48	To Peshawar in PAKISTAN
Day 49	To Rawalpindi
Day 50	To Lahore
Day 51	To Ludhiana in INDIA
Day 52	To New Delhi
Day 53	To Agra
Day 54	Explored Agra and Taj Mahal

Day 55	To Fatehpur
Day 56	To Allahabad
Day 57	To Benares
Day 58	To Holy Family Hospital, Patna
Day 59	To Muzaffarpur
Day 60	Stayed at Leprosy Hospital, Muzaffarpur
Day 61	Stayed at Leprosy Hospital, Muzaffarpur
Day 62	To Raxaul
Day 63	To Hetaura in NEPAL
Day 64	To Kathmandu
Day 65	Exploring Kathmandu
Day 66	To Raxaul in INDIA
Day 67	To Muzaffarpur
Day 68	Maintenance day in Muzaffarpur
Day 69	To Patna
Day 70	To Mirzapur
Day 71	To Jabulpur
Day 72	To Nagpur
Day 73	To Asifabad
Day 74	To Nizamabad
Day 75	To Rock Castle Hotel, Hyderabad
Day 76	To Kadiri
Day 77	To Madras
Day 78	Shipping formalities in Madras
Day 79	Stayed at Claridges Hotel, Madras
Day 80	Stayed at Claridges Hotel, Madras
Day 81	Loaded van onto SS Rajula
Day 82	Departed Madras on Rajula
Day 83	Rajula loaded onions from Nagapattinam
Day 84	Cocktails with Rajula captain
Day 85	Games of Scrabble with other passengers

Day 86	Japanese fishing vessel sighted
Day 87	Saw Sumatra on radar screen
Day 88	Landed at Penang in MALAYSIA
Day 89	Explored Penang
Day 90	To Chemor
Day 91	To Chefoo School, Cameron Highlands
Day 92	Trekked in Cameron Highlands
Day 93	To Malacca
Day 94	Arrived SINGAPORE

****

13890216R00110

Printed in Poland
by Amazon Fulfillment
Poland Sp. z o.o., Wrocław